AWAY GAME

Australians in American boardrooms

LUKE COLLINS

PREFACE

It was November in New York and I was walking south, head bowed and hands thrust in jeans pockets, wool cap firmly in place, charcoal coat unbuttoned to allow the cold air in. All I cared about was my ability to offer a warm, firm handshake to convey that vital first impression of confidence, strength and certainty. Then again, perhaps it was just a particularly male habit to worry first and foremost about your extremities.

For more than a year I had been on a slow but inexorable slide into financial oblivion. This prospect should have been of great concern, yet I had skated along and scraped by, barely working, lingering in my favourite coffee shop every day sipping US$3.50 lattes and doing the *New York Times* crossword. People assumed I was doing well — 'You had a story in *The Times*? Fantastic!' — because I *looked* healthy, indicating no work stress, comfortable in jeans and a t-shirt, newspaper tucked under my arm. I could have been one of what appeared to be thousands of New Yorkers with no discernible source of income who managed to live fabulously. Yet as the end of each month approached, my anxiety level ratcheted higher in inverse proportion to the number of days until the rent fell due.

My parents had sent money. The first time was unsolicited — I resisted and resisted and resisted every offer of financial help, even as my mother relentlessly opened her weekly phone call with: 'How are you going for money?' One day money just appeared in my bank account, and I experienced such a palpable sense of relief that I realised I had strayed to the wrong side of the fine line between pride and stupidity. The next time she asked, I put up enough resistance to satisfy myself that I hadn't exactly *asked* for help — if she hung up with the impression that some money would be useful right about now, who was I to argue? Yet living on borrowed money was living on borrowed time, and as the months ticked by I knew I had to find an alternative source of income.

Working on the theory that an uncluttered life equals an uncluttered mind, I began to shed my possessions — the digital camera, acoustic and bass guitars, electric piano, PlayStation 2, video camera. I sold the only piece of real furniture I had ever bought — an Eames plywood lounge chair — and the buyer turned out to be the paperback fiction editor at a major publishing house whose ears pricked up when I casually mentioned I was a writer. They did, I swear. I pinned his business card to the corkboard above my desk.

Two weeks and 5000 words later, my novel and dreams of a six-figure advance died after a bravura scene in which the main character wets himself in a drunken stupor at a roadside bar in New Jersey. I felt I just couldn't top that, let alone advance the story any further. Two months later I read a Richard Russo novel in which a character actually does wet himself, but I wasn't upset by Russo's lack of originality. He may have won a Pulitzer Prize, but I didn't have time to argue with him. I had a new plan to write my way out of penury: complete a screenplay in ten days flat and, once it was done, write a magazine story about how I did it. That would score me an agent — 'I have to talk to the guy who wrote the screenplay in ten days!' — which would certainly put me on the Hollywood fast track. After a lifetime of watching lousy movies and knowing I could do better, I downloaded the screenplay for *The English Patient* as a cheat sheet and got to work. My seemingly foolproof plan foundered on two crucial points: the inherent laziness that came from sitting in an apartment with access to more than 200 television channels; and a flimsy plot about a conspiracy theory that was a brazen lifting of at least four films.

'It's a spy story — just think *The Da Vinci Code* meets *The Bourne Identity*,' I imagined myself telling Hollywood studio bigwigs.

'What's with the lead character only wearing suits and black knit ties?'

'He's mourning his dead wife — that's why he's bitter and reckless. And it's a homage to the real James Bond, the original from Ian Fleming's books. This has franchise written all over it!'

Instead I trudged from my apartment to the chic Soho hotel, 60 Thompson, where my brother had arrived an hour earlier. Matthew had flown in from Melbourne for work and, shrugging off his usual horrendous jetlag, had suggested a late dinner. We hadn't seen each other for almost two years and had spoken only a handful of times since, but I was craving family and it couldn't have come at a better time: it was a couple of days before Thanksgiving, 2004. As I sat waiting for Matt in the hotel lobby, my wool cap folded in my hand and knees bobbing, I thought about the rooms above that started at around US$400 a night. My bank balance stood at US$6. If I was paying, I could have stayed at 60 Thompson for precisely 21.6 minutes.

Two years in America was meant to be enough. Like many Australians interviewed for this book, I had had no intention of staying in New York longer than that. My appointment as correspondent for *The Australian Financial Review* was initially for only a year. By the time it was extended for a second year — the newspaper having figured out just how much money it costs to maintain a correspondent in a foreign country — it still seemed as though that would be about the perfect amount of time: long enough to settle and really enjoy America, but also long enough to appreciate and crave the joys of living in Australia. As James Gorman, the Australian who now runs investment bank Morgan Stanley's global individual investor group, notes, four years seems to be the tipping point; the moment at which it becomes more difficult to return than it is to stay. I planned to return long before this.

At the newspaper in Sydney, there had been speculation for months about who would be posted to New York. We all knew the current correspondent's term was almost up; an internal email had called for applications, then ... nothing. In April 2001 I was called into the editor's office and asked whether I would like to move to New York (yes), and whether I could start within a month (you've got to be kidding!). Seven weeks later I was checking into the Malibu Hotel on Manhattan's Upper West Side, having left in such a rush that my wife had to stay in Sydney to tie up some not-insubstantial loose ends, which included vacating our apartment and selling the car.

Despite conjuring up mental images of palm trees and drinks with plastic umbrellas, the Malibu was a long way from paradise — more akin to seedier parts of Bangkok than the beaches of Koh Samui. It appeared to be the only hotel in Manhattan that crept under the newspaper's maximum accommodation cost of US$120 a night, and the reason was obvious: 'stylish and comfortable' in an 'eclectic' location was actually advertising lingo for 'cheap dive in a bad part of town'. The building was a firetrap, the neighbourhood a dodgy no-man's-land between the gentrified Upper West Side and Columbia University. Every time I returned I worried whether my bags would be gone, and it was so noisy at night that there was a clock radio offering a variety of allegedly soothing sounds to help you sleep, from birds chirping to crashing waves to wind chimes. The rumbling steam train option was presumably for New Yorkers who found themselves overnighting outside the city, kept awake by the unfamiliar, deafening silence.

On my first full day I walked from the hotel to Battery Park at Manhattan's southern tip. A friend has a theory that every day in this city offers five moments of unique craziness: as I walked the 12-mile round trip, I experienced about eighty. There were people having animated conversations with themselves, a woman carrying a rabbit in a baby sling. I saw dogs being taken for walks in prams, and dog walkers holding 15 leashes, appearing to float down the street amid a sea of labradors, German shepherds, assorted terriers and other dogs too big to keep in cramped studio apartments. Homeless men sold magazines and assorted items scavenged overnight from rubbish bins, while a man in dark sunglasses, eyes constantly scanning for police, furtively opened a briefcase containing rows of fake Rolexes while looking everywhere but at me. If a feature movie's worth of experiences wasn't provided on every block, there was at least enough for an interesting short film.

Landing in America meant a complete immersion in a culture that is superficially familiar but fundamentally foreign, and for a long time it was a thrilling exploration. I moved to the YMCA for a month before taking an apartment and being joined by my wife. Travelling about the city for work and for play, we felt like we had only each other; we were companions in a strange land where I happened to be working. Living on our private island was nice for a while, but there were already thoughts about what we would do on our return to Australia. Back to Sydney, perhaps? A house in the suburbs and kids? While we debated our future, the city diligently added layer after layer of fresh experiences until a new form emerged: the foreign became familiar and the reasons why New York City had captured imaginations for decades became clear. For all its faults — and there were too many to even begin naming them — there was an energy and vitality and a sense of opportunity that became addictive, and I began wondering exactly what I could do in Australia that could possibly compare. Writing this book has driven home one fact: you can't. It's foolish to pit America against Australia, just as it's foolish to declare one experience to be superior to the other. When the call came in early 2003 to start thinking about what I might do back in Sydney — the upshot of this conversation with my editor-in-chief was that I could return to the job I was in previously, as though time had stood still — the big bet on the United States had all but been made.

At least it had been made by me. Living on your own private island is wonderful when it's an idyllic paradise, but when the weather turns stormy there's nowhere to escape. My marriage ended in 2002, a victim of a variety of factors headed by my need to figure out who I was and what I wanted — a quarter-life crisis that had to be endured alone, without dragging another person down with me. It wasn't fair, but if I was going to fail I planned to fail on my own. In the months that followed I worked too much to be healthy and when the question of returning to Sydney was finally asked, it was hard to escape the thought that this crazily beautiful city owed me something in return.

There was something liberating about confessing the parlous state of my life to a stranger: the circumstances of my marriage break-up, my fears about ever being professionally fulfilled, the US$6 in the bank with US$1550 in rent due the following week. My brother was not a complete stranger, of course, but we were not what you would call close. Three years older than me, he had gone to boarding school when I was ten and we had since lived in different cities. I began as a journalist straight out of my Brisbane high school, where I did the minimum to get by. I completed university ten years later, having begun a degree in journalism, switched to arts, backpacked for six months, switched to law and panicked on receiving a letter warning that my existing credits would start to be deducted if I dallied any longer. I gritted my teeth and completed an economics degree, which has resulted in a full confirmation of the discipline's designation as the dismal science. Matt, on the other hand, was an indisputable genius: straight from high school to law school to a PhD, with his doctoral thesis published by Oxford University Press and now regarded as the definitive text on defamation law and the Internet. He was a barrister, lived in a fabulous house in Melbourne, and as he sat across the dinner table I had a sneaking suspicion his scarf cost more than my entire outfit.

'So why not just come home?' he asked.

It was a reasonable question, but I got the feeling he viewed my loyalty to New York as somewhat baffling given it had beaten me around the head for two years and had me in the middle of a standing knockout count. I thought about my usual reasons for why returning to Australia was not an option: aside from the embarrassment of being a professional failure, a 31-year-old divorcee with my tail between my legs, I happened to love New York. The damned place owed me a break. I had applied for a green card, and the decision was expected within eight months, so if I could only hold out ...

Yet when I replied, none of those responses emerged. There was actually no good reason to continue stumbling about in the darkness with no light at the end of the tunnel, and a steady job in Australia sure beat poverty in Manhattan.

'You're right, I should come home.'

There. I'd said it. The mental hurdle that had seemed so insurmountable actually wasn't. I just needed to understand there was no failure or success, right or wrong — just choices. With that, my parents booked me a flight home, my brother paid my rent for the month, I started contacting people in Australia about jobs, and the paralysis that had stalled my career suddenly disappeared.

A week later I met Cara. I don't mean for that to sound like a problem. While it absolutely complicated my sudden clarity, it complicated it in the loveliest way. Perhaps it was the change in my mental outlook that made the stars align: just three weeks later I spent Christmas with her family on Long Island — and realised I was counting the days before I returned home not because I was anxious to leave, but because I wanted to stay. Everything hinged on getting a decision on my green card, which I had been told to expect by the middle of 2005. I called the immigration department to notify it of my change of address.

'Yeah,' I said to the real person I reached after navigating touch-tone menus for four minutes and waiting on hold for fifteen, 'I was told a decision would take about eight months, so I want to make sure it gets mailed to me and doesn't get lost.'

'Eight months? I don't know who would have told you that.'

'What do you mean?'

'Well,' she said, 'we're currently making rulings on that green card category for applications received in 2002.'

'So when will I hear about my application?'

'Ummm ... 2007?'

I hung up, sweating. My whole plan had hinged on getting the green card and coming back to America before it really missed me. Going to Australia for six months, while not ideal, was tolerable. A year? Bad, but possible. But 2007? No way. I feared never being able to come back and I feared losing what I had found. The only solution was actually to make a living as a freelance writer, and the trip to Australia was suddenly no longer a hunt for a full-time job but a three-week dash to drum up enough work with Australian newspapers and magazines to keep me afloat in New York.

By late January 2005 I was in Sydney. It was one of those stunning sunny days that Americans imagine Australia has on a permanent basis, the kind that makes them look at you with complete incomprehension when you tell them you come from Australia.

'So ... what are you doing here?' they reply, baffled.

After meeting with a former editor I walked from Cockle Bay up Market Street, and the strangest sensation came over me: I simply didn't belong. The city was completely familiar, yet I felt like a tourist — people looked different, the accents were jarring, the atmosphere odd. I left a phone message in Manhattan, where it was early evening.

'If you were worried,' I said, 'that I might come back to Sydney, be reminded of how beautiful it is and never come back, don't be. It feels *so strange.*'

Two weeks later I experienced a palpable sense of relief at arriving 'home'. Peter Lowy, the chief executive of Westfield America, is fascinated by that defining moment when Australian expatriates realise America has become their home: after three and a half years, this was it. I couldn't wait to walk the city's streets, to be bumped and jostled and harried, to be enveloped by the subway steam that rose from the tunnels and melted the winter snow. I felt as though I had arrived in New York City anew but with the benefit of knowing exactly what to do. And when I arrived at Cara's apartment — homeless, having transferred my lease — and checked my emails for the first time in two days, there was a notification from United States Citizenship and Immigration Services.

My green card had been approved. It had taken just three and a half months.

Love often appears irrational, and that applies equally to a love of cities and countries as of people. Thousands of Australians now live and work in the United States in what might appear to be, at least at a superficial level, significantly reduced circumstances. In New York City they pay US$2000 a month to trip over each other in tiny apartments while their children and pets struggle to recall the unfamiliar sensation of walking on grass. Work pressure is often relentless and, unless you have the means, escaping the city is diffi-cult. Besides, no matter what people try to tell you, the beaches are lousy, finding a decent coffee is like striking gold, while Hershey's chocolate tastes like it is made with a glass and a half of bitterness. Yet Australians continue to come in greater and greater numbers. For all its faults, America must be doing something right.

This book relates the experiences of some of those Australians living and working here. It is not a reference guide to packing up and coming to the United States, neither does it make any recom-mendation about whether you should do so. It offers the thoughts of people who have made the transition and stayed, as well as some who have lived in America and returned to Australia. When you look past my sweeping generalisations, you'll find that all these individual experiences are unique and the stories valuable. Thank you to everyone who agreed to take time out from their busy lives to participate in this project: your generosity and frankness made my job significantly easier and more pleasurable. I hope I have returned the favour by accurately and respectfully representing your views and impressions.

Readers will be pleased to know that this is the last you'll hear of me. I once liked to think my story was vaguely interesting, but as the interviews mounted I quickly realised all lives are interesting when you begin examining the decisions people make and why they make them. I can report, however, that I still live happily in New York. My bank balance looks marginally healthier — all donations are gratefully accepted nonetheless — and I get the feeling the city may soon begin repaying my tenacity. Of course, this change in fortune may be entirely due to my decision, after a life-time of being told it only brings bad luck, to walk under every ladder I come across. Since then it's all been good.

Thank you to Sean Aylmer, my successor as New York correspon-dent for *The Australian Financial Review*, from whose lap this project fell, as well as other colleagues who have passed through or remain in this country. Thanks also to Ronnie Gramazio and everyone at John Wiley & Sons Australia for taking a chance on me.

I must thank the friends I have made since moving here who have listened with endless patience to my tales of woe, generously paid for dinner when times were shaky, allowed me to sleep on their floors, and made me appreciate the crucial role friends play in making a strange city feel like home. Thank you also to my mates in Australia, who have not forgotten me despite the weeks and months that zip by at an ever-increasing rate. When we do catch up it is as though I have never been away, and it makes me a little braver knowing you're there.

Nothing that has gone before or is still to come could happen without the love and support of my wonderful parents, Robyn and John, and my brother, Matt. If moving overseas proves who your real friends are, it absolutely proves there is nothing to compare to family. I hope I make you proud.

Finally, to Cara. Thank you.

Luke Collins

New York City

September 2005

1 ONE MILLION AUSTRALIANS

It was another hot and hazy Manhattan summer. Those with means lazed at summer homes in the Hamptons or Cape Cod, decompressing after a non-stop year. Others spent every weekday awaiting two days of rest at a crazily overpriced summer rental shared with ten others, where sleeping on the floor seemed a small price for escaping the city. The have-nots? They were stuck, sweating through the working day in the man-made sauna that is New York City, heat rising from the subway system beneath their feet and reflecting off every concrete surface.

Then there was Col Allan.

A year earlier, in 2000, Allan was prowling the fourth floor at News Limited's headquarters in Sydney's Surry Hills, home of *The Daily Telegraph*. Having spent seven years as editor of one of the country's feistiest and most influential newspapers, and a further two as editor-in-chief of *The Daily Telegraph* and *The Sunday Telegraph*, Allan was on sure ground. He was in a city he knew intimately, monitoring a political and social pulse he rarely misread. Yet unbeknown to his colleagues, Allan had a severe case of itchy feet.

'I'd effectively been doing that work for almost a decade. I won't say I had become tired of it, but I was looking for a change.'

In 1999 Allan told his then chief at News Limited, Lachlan Murdoch, that he was interested in moving into the television industry in the United States. Murdoch suggested a meeting with his father, Rupert, the chairman and chief executive of News Limited's parent company, The News Corporation Limited. News Corp, the global media giant built by Rupert Murdoch from a now-defunct news-paper in Adelaide, owns Hollywood studio Twentieth Century Fox, American free-to-air television network Fox, a host of pay television channels and assorted program development operations. If Allan wanted to jump into the electronic media, Rupert Murdoch was the man to talk to. His response was instant.

'I got on a plane and came here for a couple of days and had a meeting with Rupert, who was startled,' Allan recalls. 'He asked me how much I knew about television and my answer was zero. He indicated to me that, in his estimation, I had some skill at editing newspapers and he would prefer that I continued doing so. So I was sent back to Sydney with my tail between my legs.'

Allan toiled in Sydney for two more years, yet a seed had been planted that day, and by the time Manhattan was sweltering through 2001's long and somewhat boring summer, Allan was a few months into his new role as editor-in-chief of the *New York Post*. He had been handpicked for the job by Lachlan Murdoch, who in 1999 took responsibility for News Corp's American publications before formally becoming the *Post*'s publisher in May 2002. News Corp's flagship American publication is unquestionably the *Post*, a brash tabloid famous for headlines of the 'Headless body in topless bar' variety. It seemed a perfect fit for Allan — a publication that revelled in its status as a pugnacious underdog, an entirely entertaining cage-rattler.

As the unofficial end of the American summer, Labor Day in early September, approached, he had to admit it hadn't been a great few months. Since arriving in May, Allan had been attacked on all fronts. His appointment had been questioned: how could an Australian pos-sibly understand New York? His management style was blunt: he quickly fired two of the *Post*'s three managing editors, leaving media-watchers gasping and staff weeping on the newsroom floor. 'It was a very, very difficult period,' Allan says. 'I could have done without the pain.' Meantime he was battling to find his feet in a strange city: while Allan had spent three years in New York as a News Limited cor-respondent from 1978 to 1981, it hardly qualified him as an expert.

'I had, at least according to others, done well at the *Telegraph*,' he says. 'I felt there was an opportunity to fail here where I had not failed previously. But that's always driven me, in a way. You think about it like: do people chase success? Maybe. But I always feared failure, without being too negative about it. I didn't look so much at the opportunity of coming to the *Post* — to me it was a challenge and I didn't want to fail.'

Allan's new life came into focus on the morning of September 11, 2001.

He was at his home on the Upper West Side, getting out of the shower. 'You don't want to picture that,' he laughs, in his office on the tenth floor of News Corp's world headquarters on Manhattan's Avenue of the Americas. Typically, Allan's tie is undone and draped around his neck, his cheeks are flushed, and his stomach is showing a healthy regard for all manner of culinary and liquid delights.

'I was getting ready to go to work,' he says of that September morning. 'I always have a radio on — I'm addicted to the radio. My father bought me a crystal set when I was a child and I can't go anywhere without a radio. I had it on and the guy said, 'We've just had a report that a plane has hit the World Trade Center.' So the first thing I did, I remember, was open the window because I figured there must be a fog, and it was the most brilliant blue, clear fall morning. And I dismissed it. I thought, "They've made a mistake." '

They hadn't. Then, thinking it simply had to be an accident involving a light plane, Allan turned on the television in his bedroom. 'I called my wife and we watched the second plane hit and I remember saying to Sharon as I left, "You may not see me for a while." ' I got on the subway at 86th Street and I only got as far as 59th Street before they stopped the whole system. So I legged it from 59th Street down to here and ... holy cow.'

New York's streets were packed that morning as millions of commuters who typically used the subway system were forced to the surface. The city had closed the transit network, and police were sealing the bridges and tunnels in and out of Manhattan. People were on the streets, crowded around cars with doors open, listening to radio reports. The intersection outside News Corp's headquarters, at the corner of 48th Street, across from the Rockefeller Center, was particularly popular because of its Fox News ticker, which electronically scrolls news headlines around the building's façade. Inside, Allan was getting to work.

'People say to me, "What was it like?" and I can't remember because I just worked. I just went flat out,' he recalls. 'I think I went and had a drink at the pub at 3 o'clock that morning. I went home for a couple of hours and I was back here at 9 am, and it went on like that for weeks. We ate a lot of pizza, I know that.'

Many silver linings have emerged from the events of September 11. Allan today describes the period as 'very special'. New York gives day passes to people with money and power, but truly entering the city's consciousness usually takes years. September 11 transformed Allan's status: it endeared him to a sceptical newsroom and bonded his newspaper with a battered city. The *Post* is today an unapologetic supporter of everything and anything it views as taking the fight to those who attacked its city.

'The thing that made a difference to me was 9/11. It happened in that period,' Allan says. 'It had been one of those summers with not much going on. I'm listening, trying to understand the market, getting to know the talent at the newspaper. Then 9/11 happened and really everything changed because it gave me an opportunity. I literally worked on the backbench for three weeks. I didn't leave the backbench. I drew a lot of pages. I think it was an opportunity for the staff to see that I wasn't a back office guy; that I could copy-taste; crop pictures; draw layouts; write headlines — the things I do. It certainly helped draw the staff at the *Post* and me much closer together and I feel my relationship with the staff really changed after that.'

More than four years later Allan's footprint on the New York media landscape is obvious. The *Post* has dramatically narrowed the circulation gap on its arch-rival, the *New York Daily News*, and established itself as the unofficial barometer of the city's zeitgeist with punchy, youth-oriented features and its famous 'Page Six' gossip column. There have been many mistakes, the biggest being the front-page story naming Richard Gephardt as the running mate of the Democratic Party's 2004 presidential nominee (John Kerry actually chose fellow senator John Edwards), but each has been acknowledged with humour and honesty, helping to endear the publication to its audience. The fact that one of Lachlan Murdoch's first decisions after taking responsibility for the newspaper was to halve its cover price to US25c hasn't hurt sales either, but even the *Post*'s harshest critics agree its increased appeal is due to much more than its lower cost. Allan has a simple explanation for how he turned it all around.

'I think that personality develops. I don't think that you change it one day, you know? The *Post* has become pretty confident in itself and what it is and the way it talks to its market. I think it has become in some ways a little less conservative, which is not a bad thing. Not on fiscal issues so much, but on social issues. Rupert would probably be appalled at me saying that! It's a very liberal market and that's okay, but the thing about the *Post* is I think there are some tremendously talented young people working here and this is what I've enjoyed so much. I say that very seriously.

'I'm a reasonably blunt fellow. Generally, I've found it's an advantage, I must say. But my uncertainty about the market and my hunger to learn has improved my listening skills. The big thing that I've learnt here is to listen harder. I don't mean just to the people who are working for me, but particularly to the market. God knows, we've made errors — not just mistakes, but in tone. There's a pitch and a tone to the market. In the end, I decided to do the only thing I know how to do and that is to be instinctive. I'd contemplated editing the paper in a more consensual style because of my lack of knowledge of New York, but in the end I thought, 'Fuck it. That'll fail.' If I had any success in Sydney it was because I followed my gut.

So I decided I wasn't going to betray that, and I soon discovered I was enjoying it because I was happy.'

The editor-in-chief today sits in an office with two framed 9/11 front pages on the walls, while his wife has kept all the editions from that period in leather-bound albums, saved for posterity by the same document preservationists as the White House. A Starbucks coffee is on Allan's desk and he excitedly brandishes a photo of himself, the then publisher of the *Post*, Lachlan Murdoch, and President George W. Bush, from a meeting in the Oval Office early last year.

'I was wearing this heavy, heavy pinstripe suit and I walked into the Oval Office and I thought, "Wow." I walked in and shook Bush's hand and said, "Mr President, it's a pleasure to meet you," and he looked at me and said, "That's *some* suit you're wearing." It was great. Who would have thought it? A boy from Dubbo in the Oval Office!'

An Australian could not actually be installed in the Oval Office on a more permanent basis: the US Constitution bars people not born in the country from becoming president. Yet you will find Australians virtually everywhere else — from the boardrooms of major American corporations to university lecture halls to Hollywood movie sets. They are cooking in restaurants, pulling lattes in coffee shops and selling pies by mail order. All of them report the same thing: while they are competing in the biggest economy in the world, in a country perceived as representing the pinnacle of achievement in numerous industries, their skills are in no way inferior. In fact, Australians are excelling.

For years we have been accustomed to Americans running some of Australia's biggest companies. Telstra Corporation had Frank Blount and now has Solomon Trujillo. Westpac Banking Corporation had Bob Joss. AMP Group had George Trumbull. According to the most recent figures from the Department of Immigration and

Multicultural and Indigenous Affairs (DIMIA), as of five years ago some 4324 American executives were working in Australia as temporary residents on business visas (the corresponding number from Britain was 9631). The prevailing wisdom in many Australian corporate boardrooms seemed to favour importing management talent, perhaps on the basis that international executives have the kind of experience those who have developed domestically simply can't match.

What is less well known is that Australia has been exporting top executives to the United States for decades. These include: chairman of Philip Morris Companies (now Altria Group) William Murray, succeeded by his best friend Geoffrey Bible; Bible's long-time deputy William Webb; Jacques Nasser at Ford Motor Company; Charlie Bell at McDonald's Corporation; Douglas Daft at The Coca-Cola Company; James Wolfensohn at the World Bank. Together with Rupert Murdoch, now an American citizen, these men paved the way for a generation of Australians now working in the United States.

'Look at it: a number of the US iconic brands have been run by Australians — Coke, McDonald's, Ford, Philip Morris, News Corp and Fox — and then you've got us in the mall industry,' says Peter Lowy, the chief executive of Westfield America, the second-largest shopping mall company in the United States. 'What is more Americanised than those?'

Just as Allan found that the skills and instincts developed in Australia were the right fit for a New York newspaper, his countrymen and -women are increasingly sought after as a new generation of Australians appears within corporate America. Andrew Liveris is the president and chief executive of America's biggest chemical group, Dow Chemical. According to *Forbes* magazine, Dow Chemical was last year the ninety-third biggest company in the world (by comparison, Telstra ranked 180th). Doug Elix is senior vice president and group executive of sales and distribution at IBM. He controls operations at the computer giant that generate revenues of more than

US$80 billion a year, dwarfing Australian companies (as an example, Telstra recorded total sales of A$22.2 billion in the 2004–05 financial year). David Anstice is the president, human health, at pharmaceutical giant Merck & Co. James Gorman has just become the president and chief operating officer of investment bank Morgan Stanley's individual investor group, having formerly headed acquisitions, strategy and research at rival Merrill Lynch & Co. Greg Medcraft is the global head of securitisation at S. G. Cowen, the investment banking arm of French banking giant Société Générale. These men are among a handful of global top executives of their organisations and represent a tiny fraction of the total number of Australians living and working in the United States.

At any given time, the Department of Foreign Affairs and Trade estimates, more than one million Australians — almost five per cent of the national population — are overseas. According to figures collated in 2004 by the Sydney-based Lowy Institute for International Policy, some 760 000 Australians live overseas while 265 000 are temporarily overseas at any given time. Around 12 per cent of that total is in the United States. Although that is still only half the number in the United Kingdom and Ireland, which have traditionally had more relaxed working visa policies for Australians than the United States, figures show America is an increasingly attractive destination.

There are obvious reasons for this: English is the primary language, and Americans tend to make no effort to hide their love of all things Australian — even if they struggle to pronounce 'g'day' or 'Aussie' in anything resembling the proper way. But the two key reasons why so many Australians seem to be trying their luck in the United States are both related to the country's size and the sheer depth of its market. First, expatriates universally express a desire to test themselves against the best in the world; and second, to paraphrase the song, if you can make it in America, you can make it anywhere — and in financial terms, you can *really* make it.

The gross domestic product of the United States is about US$11.7 trillion, compared with Australia's US$631 billion. In lay terms, that means the American economy is roughly 18 times the size of Australia's. Everything to do with money in America seems big. The country's biggest company in sales terms is retailer Wal-Mart, which in 2004 recorded annual revenues of US$285.2 billion, just ahead of United Kingdom energy group BP as the world's biggest corporation. According to *Forbes* magazine's annual rankings, American companies comprise five of the world's six largest companies: Citigroup, General Electric, American International Group, Bank of America and ExxonMobil. Company size also translates into big salaries: *Fortune* magazine estimates the average compensation for chief executive officers of America's biggest 500 companies was US$10.4 million in 2004. A survey by *The Australian Financial Review* during the same period found Australia's chief executives pocketed an average of A$1.7 million a year. One interesting point is that the disparity is heavily skewed at that top end: according to recent figures, average annual earnings in the United States total about US$28 000 per person, while in Australia they are around $26 500. Given that the cost of most goods is roughly the same in both countries once the foreign exchange rate is taken into account, average earnings are almost equal.

In professions such as elite sports there is an even more obvious disconnect: the average annual salary for a Major League baseball player in 2004 was US$2.38 million, which was actually a 3.5 per cent drop on the previous year. By contrast, the total salary cap for a National Rugby League team is $3.25 million — or an average of $130 000 per player. Basketball stalwarts such as Andrew Gaze and Shane Heal can only look on in wonder when someone like Andrew Bogut comes along: picked first in the National Basketball Association draft last year, Bogut signed a multi-year deal with the Milwaukee Bucks straight out of the University of Utah. The deal is said to be worth about US$4.2 million in the first year, US$4.55 million in the second and US$4.85 million in the third year, escalating to about US$6 million in year four. Experts believe a fifth-year offer would run to about US$7.8 million. Even without taking into account an exchange rate in which one US dollar buys at least A$1.25, the numbers are mind-boggling.

Traditionally, young Australians have headed to the United Kingdom to gain overseas experience, whether simply to work in a pub for a year after finishing university or to further their careers. There are still twice as many Australians in the United Kingdom and Europe as there are in the United States. Experts see two reasons for this historical trend: the customary close relationship between the United Kingdom and Australia and, as a result of that, government policies that allow young Australians to gain working visas easily. You can readily list the famous Australians who have forged careers in Britain: feminist writer/academic Germaine Greer, author and television host Clive James, actor/satirist Barry Humphries, and pop singers such as Kylie Minogue.

Now name an Australian striding the American professional or intellectual stage. Traditionally there has been a significant barrier to entry to the United States for Australians: working visas. Before last year, any conversation between Australians living in America would inevitably turn to the visa issue — at which point the jargon would become befuddling. H1-B? EB-1? O-1? I? L-1? All are types of visas Australians live and work under in the United States. The most popular is the H1-B, which is the employer-sponsored visa held by the majority of legal foreign workers. In 2004 the US government issued 65 000 such visas worldwide, about 900 of them to Australians.

Last year the US government established a new visa called an E-3. Issued only to Australians, some 10 500 are obtainable annually. Like the H1-B, the E-3 is available to those with a bachelor's degree or higher and an offer of work in the United States. Unlike the H1-B, the E-3 allows spouses to work, thereby addressing one of the major problems faced by Australians coming to America. The fact that it is available only to Australians has been hailed on both sides as tangible proof of the close relationship between the two countries. At the press conference announcing the creation of the E-3 visa in May last year, the Minister for Trade, Mark Vaile, shied away from suggestions it could assist the so-called brain drain from Australia.

'Look, I think that we need to look at this a little bit in the reverse,' Vaile said. 'I mean, many Australian businesses are doing a lot in the United States. We're a significant investor in that economy, and Australian companies want to be able to move their professionals and their executives backwards and forwards between the United States and Australia. I'd prefer to look at it on the basis that young professionals in Australia working here have the opportunity to go into that market, expand on their skill set, get a broader experience, and obviously eventually bring those experiences back and deploy them in Australia.'

The brain drain. It is a loaded term that prompts varying reactions from both expatriate Australians and those who stay home. Some question whether Australians living in the United States are really true Australians, expressing amazement that their compatriots could possibly want to live anywhere else. Others understand the decision to move overseas but oppose it. Some fail to understand why people would leave Australia but respect their decision to do so. One thing is certain: all but a handful of Australians living in the United States miss their homeland, and nearly all, no matter where they are or how long they have been away, continue to passionately declare themselves Australian.

Bruce Stillman's response to the question 'Do you consider yourself Australian?' is emphatic: 'Absolutely. I still have very close ties to Australia. My parents still live in Sydney. I still read *The Sydney Morning Herald* every day on the web, I keep up with the football.'

Born in Melbourne, he is a Carlton supporter. 'I still keep up with what's going on in Australia and I'm still an Australian citizen. I never wanted to give up Australian citizenship.'

Stillman, it should be noted, is 52 years old and has lived in the United States for 26 years. He is married to an American and has two children born and raised in the United States who hold US and Australian passports. He is the chief executive officer of the scientific research powerhouse Cold Spring Harbor Laboratory (CSHL), based an hour north-east of New York City, and took the helm of the picturesque institution from famed scientist James Watson. In 1962 the Chicago-born Watson shared the Nobel Prize in Physiology or Medicine with Englishman Francis Crick for the discovery of the structure of deoxyribonucleic acid, or DNA. They are big shoes to fill and indicative of Stillman's ability. He came to CSHL intending to stay for just two years, but he now believes he will remain in the United States for ever, probably taking out dual citizenship. Following changes to the *Australian Citizenship Act 1948* in April 2002, Australians can now hold dual American citizenship.

'In the whole scheme of science and particularly cancer research, being head of CSHL is pretty good. It's pretty hard to beat a job like this.'

The accent? Stillman still has it. And while his office has panoramic views across Cold Spring Harbor — it is uncannily reminiscent of Sydney's northern suburbs — he keeps the real thing foremost in his mind with a big framed print of Lavender Bay and the Sydney Harbour Bridge behind his desk. Stillman left Australia primarily because there were no opportunities to conduct cancer research there: the one job he was offered in Australia after completing his initial two-year post-doctoral stint at CSHL would have involved completely switching fields to work on plant viruses at the CSIRO.

Were he starting his career today, Stillman believes he would end up in Australia. 'Things have changed a lot in Australia since the early 1980s. Unless you went back and worked for somebody else, then it was very, very difficult to go back. There weren't very many places to do research other than the Hall Institute [Walter and Eliza Hall Institute in Melbourne] or the John Curtin School. Now things are very different.'

Many Australians working in the United States find it very difficult to be enticed back, especially in a professional sense. Rightly or wrongly, Australia is seen as something approaching a retirement option: a great place to return to once your professional appetite has been sated in the United States. It is a perception that is unlikely to change so long as opportunities for career advancement remain greater offshore. One Australian executive who believes he and his wife will ultimately retire in Australia is Merck's David Anstice, who grew up in Wagga and has lived in the United States since 1988, rising to become one of the pharmaceutical giant's top executives.

'Australia had an emotional appeal, but I felt I was learning a lot more and able to contribute more here [in the US] than in Sydney. I thought, "How would life be in a big Australian company?" But because I'd already invested 15 to 20 years in a pharmaceutical company . . . it never seemed practical to flip to another company. I retain a very strong emotional attachment to Australia, but I decided that from a personal point of view I was unlikely to work there again. In a sense, I knew I had outgrown Australia — in our industry anyway. And I never really seriously contemplated throwing my hat into the ring for something else. Australia was a family, friends, lifestyle thought as opposed to a professional thought. I'm not sure that I recall one headhunter calling me throughout the 1990s, and I don't take anything from that other than there weren't any positions there.'

Various reasons are put forward for the increasing number of Australian executives in international boardrooms, particularly in America. One of the most often cited is the fact that Australian business culture has grown parallel to that in the United States, adopting many of its characteristics. Studies undertaken by leading academics on this issue such as Maastricht University Professor

Emeritus Geert Hofstede find Australia and the United States closely aligned on core business culture values: high degrees of individualism; close relationships between managers and subordinates; and solid assertiveness and competitiveness. In short, the American business model — strong multinational corporations underpinned by entrepreneurship and a vibrant small business sector — has been replicated in Australia, albeit on a smaller scale that reflects the country's significantly smaller population. Couple that with the influence of American culture and Australians' consequent comfort in dealing with that culture and you have a recipe for the development of a generation of professionals equipped to navigate corporate America with the additional advantage of a skill set many Americans lack: an international perspective and experience, a willingness to travel and step outside their comfort zones, and a level of flexibility and practicality that stems from operating in a relatively small economy where agility is crucial.

Globalisation has helped. The flattening of the international business playing field in recent years has not only opened markets for companies around the world but opened the floodgates to the flow of management ideas. Americans operating in the Australian market, such as former Telstra Corporation boss Frank Blount, introduced overtly American management philosophies into Australia, while Australians working in the United States have brought fresh ideas to corporate America. Australians no longer view ambition and leadership aspiration with as much suspicion as they once did, while Americans are adjusting to the benefits of leadership that speaks forthrightly and does what it says. Australia has a disproportionate influence when it comes to exporting ideas: while some five per cent of our national population is overseas at any given time, the percentage of Americans working internationally is significantly smaller. Indeed, the US State Department's Bureau of Consular Affairs estimated that about three million Americans are working overseas — an impressive headline number, but barely one per cent of the country's population.

Americans are increasingly recognising the benefits of international experience, and when it comes to Australians choosing between gaining experience in Europe or in the United States, the tide is beginning to turn. Australians who traditionally trod the well-worn path to London are finding the US an increasingly attractive prospect.

A former chairman and chief executive of Philip Morris, Geoffrey Bible, sees Europe and America as 'night and day' in business terms. 'A couple of characteristics I would highlight are, firstly, the size of the market and the uniformity of it,' Bible says of the United States. 'If you make a dishwasher or a washing machine, you can make it here and ship it to every state. You don't have to cross borders and show papers; it's all in English and there are no tariffs. You go into a hotel in San Francisco and the washing machine is the same as the one at home. All these things make life so much simpler than if you're trying to battle your way through to 400 million people in Europe. Europe is a magnificent part of the world and I love it. But here, from a commercial and business point of view, the *size* of the market is one advantage. If you get a product that works, your [US] market is just incredibly efficient. You can deliver it in a flash, have national marketing and advertising, and everything's on such as scale. If you're a national manufacturer here, you have enormous opportunity. That's point one.

'Point two, I would say, is you have such hard-working people here. I'll give you an example. When I was at Kraft [a Philip Morris subsidiary], we owned Oscar Mayer, the leading meats cutter — sliced meats, frankfurters. A huge company. I used to visit their plants. I went to one of their plants out in the boondocks ... these guys were working 12-hour shifts — four days on, three days off; three days on, four days off. They're on quarterly production bonus targets. They're brutal. If someone didn't turn up to work, they'd take a typist and put them on the line to make sure they hit their targets. Now that's the sort of ethic and motivating force here. You've got this very able, very willing workforce that is hard-working, competent and not unreasonable, not overly demanding — and is, in my view, by and large well treated. I think that's an enormous plus.'

The flow also goes the other way: while Australians are increasingly coming to the United States, there are now abundant jobs attracting skilled workers to Australia. According to DIMIA, while the net loss of skilled Australians in the five years to 2003 was approximately 135 000 people, the net number of skilled foreign workers coming to Australia totalled 302 000. The problem is that the brain drain — for want of a better term — seems to be concentrated at the very top of the corporate and intellectual tree, so the question becomes just how the flow of professionals to overseas destinations can be stemmed by a country with a small population base, a mid-sized economy, comparatively smaller companies, and more limited access to the volume of capital needed to foster growth and entrepreneurship. In that respect, a solution is elusive.

'You've got to accept that if you want to go home it's probably a different focus,' says New York City–based Greg Medcraft, of S. G. Cowen. 'I think you're choosing the balance between lifestyle and your career. At some point in your life, you want lifestyle more than making money. I think when you choose that is when you head back to Australia.'

The balance is changing, however.

'Increasingly companies are looking for Australians who have worked offshore,' Medcraft says. 'We've been repatriating Australians who have worked overseas. It has become a much more fluid market. What we try to do at SocGen [Société Générale] is if they're good people and they want to go now, we try to find them a job and give them a chance to go back.'

Yet even those who have been closely associated with Australia — who have, to an extent, driven the country's political and cultural agenda — at times find it hard to imagine returning. Most believe they eventually will, but many also fear it will be something of a letdown, a case of settling for something less exciting.

'I worked very hard because I didn't want to screw up and I didn't want to be sent home with my tail between my legs because I hadn't done well,' says the *New York Post*'s Allan of his first few months in America. 'At the same time, it dawned on me that I had probably taken on a more significant a challenge than I thought I had. I remember being here for a year and looking forward to going down to Sydney, and we went, and it was great fun. I always enjoy going there. Sydney is truly one of the great cities in the world. But I don't find it as intellectually stimulating as New York. I'll be criticised for that, but it's true.'

2 A BIGGER SEA

In 1992, straight out of high school, Poppy King invested $40 000 to create her eponymous line of cosmetics after being unable to find a long-lasting matte lipstick. The month of the launch, Poppy products appeared in *Australian Vogue*, and the company was turning a profit within three months. By 1994 annual revenues were headed towards $6 million. King's products seemed to be everywhere — as was Poppy herself — and were even being sold in Barneys New York, a store that epitomises style in one of the world's most fashionable cities. In 1995 King was named Young Australian of the Year. She appeared to be living proof that Australian products and personalities could go out and conquer world markets. It was a remarkable rise, and to many it seemed too good to be true.

Perhaps it was. With the business financially stretched and requiring capital to expand into the United States and develop secondary products such as lingerie, in 1997 Tab and Eva Fried injected $3.5 million into Poppy Industries, taking a 50 per cent stake in the company. The relationship between King and the Frieds soured after little more than a year, and in August 1998 the Frieds resigned as directors. The company fell into receivership a month later. In December, however, the heir to the Harris Scarfe department store chain, Adam Trescowthick, came to the rescue and reinstated King as chief executive after paying receivers $1.3 million for the company. Trescowthick took 80 per cent of Poppy Industries, leaving King with 10 per cent, the remaining 10 per cent being held by the former chief executive of Kerry Packer's Publishing & Broadcasting Ltd, Peter Yates.

The reprieve was short-lived. Trescowthick was battling problems on other fronts: in 2000 Harris Scarfe, once Australia's third largest retailer, collapsed under debts of $180 million and found itself under an Australian Securities and Investments Commission spotlight. Trescowthick, who joined the company in 1990 after graduating from Monash University with a business degree, rising to general manager by 1996, later admitted that accounting was 'not my strong point'. The news was no better at Poppy Industries. It went into receivership in 1998 and the death spiral finally ended in late 2002, when US cosmetics giant Estée Lauder Companies bought the Poppy trademark for a figure rumoured to be as much as $2 million. The lipstick range that made King's name was discontinued.

King still wears her trademark flame red lipstick, but today she works not for herself but for Estée Lauder in New York. At around the same time that Poppy Industries finally ceased trading, Estée Lauder hired King as vice president of product development, colour, on its Prescriptives brand. After enduring years of negative publicity about her business activities and personal life, King leapt at the opportunity to leave Australia.

'One of the big drawbacks and/or comforts of Australia — even though I probably couldn't have articulated it at the time — is that it's a very risk-averse country in every aspect other than sport,' says King, sitting in New York's Four Seasons Hotel. 'When it comes to risk in personal life or professional life ... Australia's just not very conducive or celebratory of people who take risks, whereas in America, in general there is an admiration for people who are willing to take a risk.'

King quickly points out that throughout its travails, which she describes as a 'very difficult period', Poppy Industries never actually ceased trading. Yet Estée Lauder, founded in 1946 by Estée Lauder and her husband Joseph and not known for risk-taking, showed no hesitation in hiring King despite her company's fate.

'I think they see that as a rite of passage in business. The attitude over here was, "Of course your business hit the wall. How old were you? Twenty-seven?" In Australia, it was like I was an elected official and let down a public office. I made it very clear to the most senior people in the Lauder Corporation that my business hitting the wall was not unconnected to my own mistakes. It wasn't something that just kind of happened independent of me. And they were fine with that.'

King had been visiting New York at least twice a year since 1993, when Barneys began carrying her products. While she admits it sounds clichéd, the first time she visited the city as an adult she knew she wanted to live there. 'I've been lucky enough to have travelled to lots of beautiful cities, but this is the only city I've really thought, "I want to live here."' King formally moved to New York in October 2002 but was in the city during the September 11 terrorist attacks. She was not deterred.

'It's the sense of opportunity, definitely,' King affirms. 'No two days are the same, no two subway rides are the same. There's something incredibly levelling about the place in the sense that no matter how rich you are, no matter how successful you are, you still have to deal with all the inconveniences of New York and the loud noise and the traffic. It has this strange combination of being very levelling and humbling as well as being very uplifting and omnipotent. It's just this strange combination that particularly appeals to me. There's that sense that you could turn a corner and it could change your life.

'I definitely viewed it as a new chapter in my career. At that time I was actually thinking about the next stage for me from a career perspective. I was interested in a new challenge, and whereas most people go from being in a corporation to starting their own business, I was interested in doing it the other way around — in ostensibly doing the same thing, the thing I love, but doing it in a new country in a new structure. Had the position been in another city, I'm not quite sure. The fact it was based in New York made it a no-brainer for me. That was just, you beaut!'

Perhaps the motivation for King to move to the United States seems obvious: after several tough years professionally and personally, it promised a fresh start and the opportunity for relative anonymity. While Australians seek opportunities in the United States for numerous reasons, King's motivation is not unique at a more fundamental level: many expatriates seem to harbour a deep desire to test themselves in the world's biggest economy against people perceived to be the best at what they do.

Although being successful in your given professional field in Australia can be tremendously rewarding — both financially and in terms of lifestyle — the analogy many draw is that essentially you will always remain a big fish in a small pond. Consider Australia's richest man: Kerry Packer. While he is easily the country's wealthiest individual — *BRW* magazine estimated his worth at A$6.9 billion last year — he would rank only ninety-fourth in *Forbes'* 2005 list of the world's richest people (the richest, Microsoft Corporation co-founder Bill Gates, with an estimated net worth of US$46.5 billion, could buy Packer almost ten times over). Even Australia's most successful business export, Rupert Murdoch, bowed to that inevitability in late 2004 by formally moving his News Corporation empire to the United States after more than half a century in Australia. The big pond is the United States: no other country is wealthier, no other country can claim to be the world centre for so many industries, and no other country can boast the sheer number of dominant companies and top professionals in those fields.

For photographer Ben Watts, America represented the logical next stage in his career. The elder brother of actress Naomi Watts, he was born in London but finished high school in Australia after his family moved to Sydney in 1982. After studying visual communications at the Sydney College of the Arts while taking photographs on the side, Watts quickly found work at emerging magazines such as Mushroom Pictures boss Martin Fabinyi's *Follow Me Gentlemen*. But it wasn't enough and Watts arrived in New York in 1995 with high hopes, his portfolio of photographs and no work.

'America was the next step,' he says. 'I felt that it was time to fly the nest — I'd done what I could do in Australia and, as beautiful as it is, I wanted to go, I wanted to see it, I wanted to test my skills. So I came over here.' Despite his solid body of magazine work in Australia, it was Watts' more experimental college photographs that landed him his first American commission — for global sportswear goliath Nike.

'America has already got [famed photographers] Steven Miesel, Mario Testino — the biggest of everything in the world is right here in New York,' Watts says. 'So if you come, you've got to bring something different to the table. If you show up with what's already been served, you're not going to get any respect. You might get a career out of imitating — you have to be lucky even for that — but you really need to show up with something original. In some ways, I wish I'd gone to London. London is a powerhouse of creativity. But I'd already decided I wanted to come here because it was novel to me and I was very much into hip-hop music and culture, so I came here. And things worked out for me.'

Watts now shoots celebrities such as musician Sheryl Crow and rapper Snoop Dogg for magazines including *Esquire*, *GQ* and *Vanity Fair*. He has published a book called *Big Up*, which highlights the unique melding of hip-hop music and popular culture in his work. And there is not even a hint of complacency, despite success that takes him all over the world and has provided a lifestyle that includes a New York City base and a beach house in Montauk, the laid-back holiday destination you reach after driving through the hyper-expensive towns that make up the Hamptons, at the eastern tip of Long Island.

'You're only as good as your last shoot, as they say. And it's very, very stiff competition here,' Watts says. 'They're always ready to substitute you, so you have to make sure you're on the field and playing well. You're self-employed. So I could pack up my cameras, walk out of here today and do a disastrous photo shoot, do another not so good one, then an average one and seriously harm my career. I could go through some sort of crisis. Nothing is guaranteed. It's important not to become complacent. I'm all about being content but not complacent; when you become complacent, people know. They can see when you're not making an effort. And the whole thing about being in America, speaking frankly and honestly, is the financial reward — and when there's a financial reward, there's a selection of great talent there. So you want to make sure that, just like any business, you're providing good service and you're seen to be doing that. As shallow as some things might seem, I think people really do respect hard work.'

The desire to pit yourself against the best of the best manifests not only in creative fields — with actors flocking to Hollywood, photographers and advertising executives to New York, and journalists all over the country — but also in the business world. After six years at rival Merrill Lynch, where he finished as head of acquisitions, strategy and research, James Gorman has just taken the role of president and chief operating officer of investment bank Morgan Stanley's individual investor group. Gorman was known to be close to Merrill Lynch's chief executive officer, Stanley O'Neal, and was seen as a potential future head of the company. He has now assumed a similar position at Morgan Stanley, having been hand-picked by the man recently appointed to turn the organisation around, John Mack. Gorman's explanation for being in the United States is simple: he came to New York from Melbourne to study at Columbia Business School, and never left.

'I thought I'd come back to Australia. I was pretty sure I'd come back. But I wanted the experience of an international qualification, partly to test myself against people from around the world, and also to learn particularly from the business community here and the tremendous access to Wall Street. You simply couldn't get that in Australia at the time.'

Raised in Melbourne, Gorman was working as a lawyer when he decided the business world was his true calling. After a short stint with management consulting group McKinsey & Company, Gorman arrived in Manhattan in August 1985 to do a Master's of Business

Administration at Columbia University, one of America's top-ranked 'Ivy League' colleges — a list that includes Harvard, Yale, Brown and Princeton.

'I was a lawyer and I knew that I wanted to be in the business community,' he says. 'My perception, rightly or wrongly, was that it would be difficult to make that transition without having any business skills or background. I decided getting an MBA would give me the credentials. I wasn't worried that I would be unable to do the work; it was getting the credentials for somebody to give you a chance to make the switch. And the MBA did that.'

Why New York? At the time, Gorman says, there were few options for studying business in Australia aside from the Australian Graduate School of Management — a joint venture between the University of New South Wales and the University of Sydney — and the Melbourne Business School at the University of Melbourne.

'While there were then some very small business school programs in Australia … they were very small and not very global, not very linked to the global financial markets, which is where I was focused. It's hard to get anywhere in the world to replicate what we have here. The first two years it was mercenary: I was here to earn US dollars to pay off my college debt. It was that simple. I had a US dollar debt and I was earning US dollars, and I thought I would do that for probably two years and then return home. I was given increased responsibilities and I felt that I could compete with people around the world and I was single, so I kind of just took the opportunities where they fell and they happened to fall squarely in New York. It had nothing to do with a desire to live in America — I was pretty sure I'd come back. But it just didn't turn out that way.'

In some respects, stories such as Gorman's and that of the chief executive of Cold Spring Harbor Laboratory, Bruce Stillman, are unusual in that they have built careers in the United States essentially from scratch. Stillman arrived in America in 1979 to do post-doctoral work — and 26 years later he is still here, running one of the country's most respected scientific research institutes. But he insists that while a desire to test himself against the world's best scientists and researchers was a motivating factor, it 'wasn't necess-arily the driving force for me to leave Australia'.

'The reality is, I think, that overseas experience is essential to get a job in Australia,' says Stillman of his particular field. 'At least it was then. Having overseas post-doctoral experience was a big plus. Having broad experience in different places is better than not having moved. I know people who are working at the ANU [Aus-tralian National University in Canberra] who just never left there, and they're doing OK, but they're not doing the work others are. I think there are a lot of opportunities in the US.'

Stillman believes that is changing and is quick to add that it is 'possible, if you're very, very good, to do research as good as here in Australia'. However, once again, America's depth — particularly financially through its strong philanthropic culture — is critically significant. It is hard to underestimate the impact of America's phil-anthropic culture, which critics suggest is a response to inadequate government funding. Regardless of the catalyst, the numbers are staggering: according to the National Philanthropic Trust (NPT), almost nine in ten American households donate money, and the average given annually is US$1620. In 2003 total donations were US$240.72 billion; public giving has increased in 39 of the past 40 years and it is estimated there will be some US$6 trillion in charitable bequests between 1998 and 2052. As of August 2005, the NPT — an independent public charity dedicated to increasing philanthropy — claimed religious and faith-based groups were the recipients of US$88 billion in donations in 2004, followed by edu-cation (US$33.8 billion), health (US$22 billion), human services (US$19.2 billion), and arts, culture and humanities (US$14 billion). Some universities are sitting on mind-boggling amounts of money: Harvard has an endowment of more than US$25 billion (it is the second biggest non-profit organisation in the world after the Bill and Melinda Gates Foundation). Yale has more than US$12.5 billion and Princeton more than US$8 billion. That kind of money can fund a lot of university places for poorer students, not to mention research and development operations.

'The US dominance in medical research is going to be challenged,' Stillman says. 'But it's still the best, finance-wise and research-wise. It's still one of the top countries in the world, and I think part of the reason for that is philanthropic support of science. It's the philanthropy that gives you the money to do the really innovative things.'

While some Australians, such as *New York Post* editor-in-chief Col Allan, enter America's journalism industry at or near the top, many more discover what it is like to begin at the bottom. Belinda Luscombe today sits in an office in New York City's historic Time & Life Building, which is technically part of the Rockefeller Center but was the first building in that precinct to cross Sixth Avenue. While media giant Time Warner has moved to its striking new headquarters at the south-west corner of Central Park, the publications that are part of its magazine division, Time Inc, have remained in the Time & Life Building. It simply had too much history for them to consider leaving — Marilyn Monroe detonated the dynamite for the building's first excavation in 1957, and it was completed in 1959, although it seems as if it is in a permanent state of internal renovation as offices shift and piecemeal improvements are made.

In a comfortable, glass-walled office, Luscombe is a long way from Sydney and a long way from her first job in New York. Holding a Bachelor of Arts in English literature and a Diploma of Education from the University of Sydney, Luscombe arrived in the city in 1991 after spending two years covering education news at *The Daily Telegraph-Mirror* in Sydney, the tabloid newspaper ultimately owned by Rupert Murdoch's News Corporation that later became *The Daily Telegraph*. Luscombe quickly discovered just how much weight her experience had in the world's media capital.

'That was kind of the equivalent of working for the Cat Fancier Association magazine of Woop Woop,' she quips. 'It meant nothing to them. I had a few hopes for the [*New York*] *Post* because Murdoch owned it. But there weren't many Australians there then. I made a few calls to the papers but I wasn't brave and you really have to be very ballsy or lucky to get in here. Coming to New York City from Australia — I was 27 — was like taking two years back, going right back to the beginning of your professional career. It was like going back to the beginning.'

Luscombe's architect husband was in New York on a fellowship, so the couple could make ends meet.

'New York very quickly makes you very, very hungry because you realise it's so much harder than anything you've had to do,' Luscombe says. In 1991 the US publishing industry was going through a tough period. 'No one was buying advertising and so the industry itself was receding. It was not hiring.'

She soon found herself having tea with, and receiving advice from, fellow expatriate Victoria Roberts, an illustrator whose work appears in *The New Yorker* and countless other publications. 'Early on I did a story on Australian women in New York and met Victoria Roberts ... and she said if you just want to do the professional equivalent of lifting up this teacup, you have to know that 2000 other people want to do that as well. It's just so competitive. So if you're competitive, which I am ... I just started at the bottom and worked my way up.'

Her first job was as a receptionist in an architecture office. That lasted about eight weeks. A contact then put her back in the journalism game with a job at a trade newspaper called *Magazine Week*, 'a magazine about magazines'.

'I did that for about six to eight months and did okay — showed some, I guess, showed some spunk. And then I got hired just by a fluke to be at an in-house magazine here [a staff publication at Time Warner called *FYI*]. I ran that for a couple of years, and the good thing about that was you got to meet all the editors

2 A bigger sea

and you got to show off a lot and eventually [in 1995] they hired me to edit the people page here at *Time* magazine. I was completely elated.'

Luscombe's first job at *Time* was as a staff writer and 'people' columnist. She became a senior editor in April 1999 and was named to her current role as arts editor in January 2003. Just a month later the first US issue of *Time Style & Design* was released under her editorship. Her position as arts editor means she directs cultural coverage at one of the world's most widely read and respected news magazines, a broad brief that includes everything from movies and music to architecture, ballet and books. While she has been offered good jobs back in Australia — including, it is rumoured, the editorship of *Good Weekend*, the insert magazine distributed weekly by *The Sydney Morning Herald* and *The Age* — she has no plans to return. At least, not yet.

'I really wanted to go do change-the-world kind of stuff,' Luscombe says of her desire to work overseas. 'I assumed New York would be the first stop on some kind of life of lots of travel. Maybe we'd go somewhere else after this. I did tell my mother, "It's just going to be two years". My life changed, particularly because I'm in one of those jobs where people are contractually obligated to suck up to me … it's nice to be sucked up to. Who wouldn't want that? It's better than having to do the sucking up.'

What if you are at the next level — working within an organisation and asked to come to the United States to push your career along? For many it is a difficult decision to make: there are competing factors such as partners, children, family and friends, not to mention giving up the familiarity of Australia and a relatively prestigious position for the uncertainty of the international corporate greasy pole. Yet thousands of Australians have made the choice, including the president of human health at pharmaceutical giant Merck, David Anstice. Born in Wagga Wagga in New South Wales, Anstice worked at the Australian Pharmaceutical Manufacturers Association (APMA), now Medicines Australia, for five years before joining Merck in 1974 and had always harboured a desire to work overseas.

'Prior to joining the APMA I had planned to work with them for two to three years and then work in Europe,' he says. 'After my experience growing up in the 1960s, if you will, my orientation was to Europe rather than the US. But I was fortunate because I was in a truly global industry — I didn't know how fortunate I was.'

Anstice had dealt with Merck in his role at APMA. He was ready for a change, and he believed American corporations had some unique attributes.

'They seemed to be more energetic, less hidebound, less worried about who you were and much more concerned about what talents you could bring. I found their view of the world very refreshing and truly global. So I think when I joined Merck I did so probably for three reasons: not necessarily so I could travel, but I felt I would learn a lot by being part of a global company, that it would open my mind up a lot more; I saw American companies in general and Merck specifically as being very receptive to new ideas and new approaches; and it had a high energy level and was about how good you were. That was a critical element.'

Merck is also known internationally as Merck Sharp & Dohme and operates around the globe. In 2004 it recorded annual sales of US$22.9 billion, and while it has attracted headlines for its voluntary withdrawal of osteoarthritis medicine Vioxx following heart and stroke concerns, it boasts many other products including post-menopausal osteoporosis treatment Fosamax, male hair loss drug Propecia and high-cholesterol medicine Zocor. Anstice now sits on the company's 11-member management committee — a long way from where he joined the company in 1974. Yet even then he quickly began to realise the potential his new employer offered.

'I started to get good experience from 1977 onwards. I got a marketing job that was senior enough for me to be invited to some of the regional meetings we had. I think there was more personal growth. At that time, I didn't have any notions that I would be called to run our business in Australia. I was only interested in learning.'

Anstice first came to the United States in 1981 to participate in a Merck development program. 'My wife will tell you I'm probably more ambitious than I myself think, but I did believe the thought of living in a different country and experiencing something very different was exciting and I saw it as very individually fulfilling. And it was billed as a two-year development program, so there seemed to be little downside risk. I kind of said yes in about ten seconds.'

Merck was beginning to take notice of Anstice and plot his future. Just nine months into what was meant to be a two-year stint, the company started talking to him about going to South Africa, a country at that time beset with unrest as the anti-apartheid movement gained momentum ahead of the release in 1990 of Nelson Mandela after 27 years in prison and the lifting of the ban on the African National Congress (ANC) and other political groups opposed to the ruling National Party. The ANC overwhelmingly won free elections in 1994 and has been in power ever since. 'So I barely got a taste of the US and was suddenly contemplating living in another country,' Anstice says. 'And it was a country that had a lot of social and political issues. I don't particularly recall thinking I'd like to extend it [the time in the US] at that time. The main issue was my new wife: when I mentioned South Africa to her, she said, "Are you crazy?"'

Suffice to say, they went. Anstice ran the company's South African operation before returning to Australia in 1984 and then became Merck's country manager in 1987. Just two years later came an offer to relocate to the company's global headquarters in Rahway, New Jersey. (Rahway is near Newark Airport, but Merck has since moved to Whitehouse Station, New Jersey, about 70 kilometres west of Manhattan.) It was a difficult decision: Anstice was happy running Merck's Australian arm, while his American wife, Ana-Maria V. Zaugg, had joined management consultancy McKinsey & Company in 1984.

'I became country manager for our business in Australia at the age of 37 and then I got offered this job opportunity in the US when I was 39. I turned 40 the month before I got here. In fact, I remember thinking, "This [running the Australian operation] is one of the best jobs in the company and I could continue doing this and growing and learning for the next ten years." Getting the job offer was probably a bit off-putting because I wasn't ready. My wife was working at McKinsey in Australia and she really enjoyed living and working there. She said, "It's 100 per cent your decision. If you tell me you don't want to go to the US, that's fine with me. You're not hearing me now and you won't hear me in the future saying I want to go back to the US. I'm very happy here and if we spend the rest of our days here, that's fine with me." She said it was my call and offered to buy one-way tickets home if I turned around after a couple of months and said I didn't like the US. If we had children, I don't think we would have been going to America.

'The impression you have often is that this is the major leagues, and part of my motivation in leaving Australia was I couldn't stay in Australia forever in the job I had at that time. There was going to be a point in time when either I got bored or they got bored with me. I think ten years is probably a long time for any one person to lead a country operation. At some point I think you lose the energy for that job. And even after ten years I would have been only 47, so hardly ready to go into retirement. The two motivations were I couldn't stay in that job forever and I was interested in seeing how I handled things in a different league. That was quite motivational. A big part of my motivation was just how good is good? The US is very competitive; it draws on a huge population. I wanted to see whether the skills I had were up to it.'

Challenge and opportunity, however, do not totally offset the gravity of the decision to leave Australia, or the nervousness it can arouse.

'The moment I accepted that job I knew I could be back in Australia in 12 months but it wouldn't be in this company,' Anstice says. 'It was either leaving Australia for an extended period or, if I was back in Australia any time soon, it would be without Merck.'

Doug Elix faced similar circumstances. Elix is today one of computing group IBM's top managers. As senior vice president and group executive for IBM's worldwide sales and distribution operations, he leads divisions that account for annual sales of about US$80 billion in products and services. He is on his second stint in the United States with the company. As with Anstice, the first (in 1981) came about through the company's internal development program.

'I was an underling in those days,' Elix recalls from the company's global headquarters in Armonk, about an hour north of New York City. 'It gave us a great taste of how it worked and how people behaved, so when we had the opportunity to come again, which we did in 1996, it wasn't a difficult decision.'

His motivation for initially coming to America, he says, was purely 'a means to an end: advancing my career'.

'The international assignment, for me, was a means of moving my career forwards. I then learnt the personal advantages ... and the sort of expanding you can do, personally, from an international assignment.'

Elix returned to Australia and worked his way up through the company's ranks before being asked in 1990 to move to Japan and manage IBM's financial services business across the Asia–Pacific.

'I learnt a lot about another culture. It was a fabulous business experience,' he says. 'I don't think you can be a good senior executive in an international or global company any more without one or more experiences of working internationally. As world business globalises more and more, executives who have international experience, are used to working in different cultures and know how to get things done become more and more valuable. When you look at our top 50 executives, you have representation from all over the world. It's very important.'

In 1994 Elix was named chief executive officer of IBM Australia. Two years later he and his wife were finally nearing the end of renovations to their Sydney home and preparing for an extended stay in Australia when the company called.

'I can remember well getting the phone call. I had just finished building onto my house,' he recalls. 'They were about to lay carpet in a new part of the house and my wife looked at me when I said, "When do I start?" I took on the job of president of ISSC, which finally became IBM Global Services. It was a great opportunity.'

In December 1996 Elix became the general manager of IBM Global Services' North American operation, the business and information technology arm of the company. Two years later his brief was expanded to cover the Americas — taking in the United States, Canada and Latin America — and in October 1999 he was named senior vice president and group executive of IBM Global Services worldwide. In that position, he oversaw businesses boasting 170 000 staff in 160 countries with total annual revenues of US$36 billion. Elix took on to his latest role in May 2004.

'I think Australia is a wonderful country. I love it when I'm there and I love working there,' he says, speaking of the dilemma he faced when asked to leave Australia and continue his career in the United States. 'I guess I figured if I was going to stay with IBM, I was probably going to stay here until I retire. There wasn't much left for me at IBM in Australia.'

It is tempting to think that while people beginning their careers or halfway up the professional ladder are afflicted with doubts about leaving Australia for an uncertain future, those at the top of the tree suffer no such dilemmas. After all, it should be easy: you are stepping into a top job and your company is paying all your expenses. You are pampered and have the means to return home whenever you like, depending on your schedule. Yet top executives face the same issues as everyone else, particularly when they already have comfortable lives in Australia.

Bob Isherwood first left Australia in the early 1960s, part of a wave of Australians that landed in the United Kingdom during that decade, among them Germaine Greer, Clive James, and the men who transplanted the satirical magazine *Oz* to London in 1967 — social commentator and author Richard Neville and artist and film-maker Martin Sharp. Isherwood was actually on his way to the capital of Italy's picturesque Umbria region to study at Perugia University for Foreigners, but ran out of money and ended up at art school in England.

'I came to England because people spoke English and at that time I think there might have been a bigger brain drain to England than to the US for Australians. I'd like to say I was part of a generation coming out of Australia at a time when it was a great environment for producing creative people because of the big blue sky and the way of life and the feeling that nothing here has been done before. But once these people were created, they weren't actually very well received by Australians generally.'

Isherwood's plan was to spend two years working in the United Kingdom before returning to Australia, which was then considered to have one of the world's highest standards of living — surely more appealing than dark and dank London.

'I was told by a couple of respected people that if I was to spend two years abroad, I could double my salary when I got back to Australia,' he says. 'A lot of Australians did it at that time. But I found if you got past the two-year stage, you tended to stay for a long time. I stayed for 17 years.'

The reason for that extended period in London was simple: Isherwood was relishing being challenged professionally. 'I wanted to be one of the world's best, and you have a better chance of getting there when you work with the people who are already there,' he says. 'You work with the people and in the places that help you do great work.'

Finally returning to Australia in 1982, Isherwood created the Sydney advertising agency Campaign Palace, setting the industry alight with innovative creative work for clients including Holeproof and Ansett, and garnering numerous domestic and international awards in the process. When Bates Worldwide, then owned by Saatchi & Saatchi, bought Campaign Palace in 1986, Isherwood moved across. Founders Maurice and Charles Saatchi left the company in 1995. The following year Isherwood became global creative director. Today he divides his time between his house in Miami and his glass-enclosed office at Saatchi & Saatchi in Lower Manhattan with views to the Statue of Liberty. A glass wall separates him from the firm's worldwide chief executive officer, New Zealander Kevin Roberts, and Isherwood confesses the men are joined at the hip. Despite being in his sixties, Isherwood plans to retire only when Roberts does.

When he began as global creative director, Isherwood tried to work from Sydney, but the demands of overseeing the creative content of an agency working around the globe and around the clock forced him to reconsider. 'It was very, very hard,' he says of working from Sydney. 'I relocated back to London again and I was there until I came here.'

There was one hiccup: Isherwood and his American wife, who was about to give birth at the time, saw New York City's World Trade Center twin towers collapse before their eyes from their living room on September 11, 2001. It forced the couple back to Australia — their daughter was born in a hotel — and rekindled Isherwood's determination to work from Sydney.

'We watched the whole thing,' he says of the twin towers' collapse. 'At that point we went back to Australia for a while because it was so crazy here, particularly where we were and where our offices are, and we couldn't go back to our apartment. We went back to Australia, and that was fantastic, but in December I had to come back to New York three times. That was a killer.'

So they returned to the United States.

'I think when you're away for a long time, although I feel passionately Australian, at the same time I don't feel I'm physically rooted there, if you know what I mean,' says Isherwood. 'I think I can probably live anywhere, which is something that happens to you when you travel a lot. I don't get homesick but I always feel great when I'm home. You can't compare them — there's no like for like. You have to just take the best out of each place.'

3 THE WHOLE WORLD AT YOUR FEET

Every few months — roughly three or four times each year — The Beverly Hills Hotel takes a distinctly Australian turn. If you are not distracted by the celebrities milling around the pink-walled hotel's lobby or lounging in private cabanas by the pool, you will find a handful of the top Australians in the entertainment industry gathering for their regular lunch at The Polo Lounge, the famous watering hole for generations of Hollywood haves and want-to-haves. The group's nickname varies — some like 'Gumnut Mafia' or 'The Irregulars'. They eat, drink, reminisce and try to bring a little bit of Australia to Los Angeles, a city that at times can seem as though it's on another planet entirely.

'We don't gather around the piano and sing songs about Bondi, but we do get together three or four times a year,' says Greg Coote, formerly the managing director of Village Roadshow in Australia for 12 years, managing director of the Ten Network television group and founding executive director of the first FM radio licence in Australia, Sydney's 2DAY-FM. He now runs the Los Angeles–based Coote/Hayes Productions.

Coote/Hayes Productions was formed when Coote, then president and chief executive officer of Village Roadshow Pictures, and Jeffrey Hayes, then president of Village Roadshow's television division, undertook a management buyout of Village Roadshow's television operations. Since its inception, the company has specialised in television work, completing more than $500 million worth of productions in Australia in recent years, including the award-winning mini-series *On the Beach*.

Coote is one of The Polo Lounge group's founding members, having lived in the United States since 1986. Others include David Hill, the sports production legend who is now president of satellite company DirecTV's entertainment group (part of Rupert Murdoch's News Corporation); David Evans, the former chief executive officer of television station GTV Nine in Melbourne, now president and chief executive officer of Crown Media Holdings and a director of newspaper group John Fairfax Holdings, publisher of *The Sydney Morning Herald* and *The Age*; David Lyle, the former head of development and acquisitions for Channel Nine who is now the chief operating officer of Fox Reality Channel; Bruce Davey, actor Mel Gibson's partner in Icon Productions; Malcolm Dudley-Smith, the executive vice president of sales and business development at Warner Television; and Ric Birch, the man behind the spectacular opening and closing ceremonies at the Sydney Olympics, among many other major events. The non-entertainment industry member is Walter Mariani, Qantas Airways' senior executive vice president for the Americas. The attendee list expands whenever Australian-based entertainment industry executives are passing through town.

'All the television executives come in May and we will host a dinner somewhere for those guys,' Coote says.

If you think this sounds like a bunch of Australians getting together for a debauched liquid lunch, you would be right — at least in spirit.

'We said we would,' DirecTV's David Hill says of a recent gathering that promised to show Americans what real drinking looks like. 'This was the twenty-sixth Hollywood Aussie Irregulars and we said we were going to celebrate the great Friday lunch and we were going to get hammered, and of course we didn't. We make a great show of having a beer when we sit down and then reality sets in and we realise we've all got meetings all afternoon and we say, "Um, I might just have an iced tea now." It's pathetic. It's absolutely pathetic.'

That said, Hill has no confusion about the real purpose of the gatherings: 'We get together once every three or four months and it's kind of like you've never left Sydney. You sit down and everyone gossips.'

It isn't a huge group of people. The 65-year-old Evans, who is on his way back to Australia permanently, is quick to note that the number of his compatriots working in Hollywood has remained pretty static in recent years, although observers might be forgiven for thinking otherwise given the headlines generated by the work of actors such as Nicole Kidman, Naomi Watts, Heath Ledger, Geoffrey Rush, Eric Bana and the New Zealand–born Russell Crowe. At the business end of the Hollywood spectrum, the pickings are much slimmer.

'There's not a hell of a lot of us. We're not talking dozens of people,' Evans says. 'If you're talking executives, then the number really hasn't increased over the years. Looking across the spectrum, I'm quite sure the number of Australians has increased quite dramatically. I think there are a lot of people in Australia who would like to make the move, but it's not an easy move to make. I'm not quite sure how I did it. I'm really not.'

Evans had a foothold in the Australian television industry when he decided, at the age of 27, to move to Toronto to gain more experience.

'When I went back to Australia, I'd stayed away for not much longer than a year, but it proved to be a very valuable experience in terms of moving up the ladder.' Back then, he says, gaining overseas experience seemed the best way of advancing in the television industry. After working his way up for several years, Evans spent seven years — until the mid 1980s — running Channel Nine in Melbourne for Kerry Packer. Still his feet were itchy.

'I wanted to do a bit more with my life. I'd got to the point in Australia where I'd been doing that job for a number of years and what was there left to achieve? I yearned for more experience in an industry that I really enjoyed working in. My wife was an American, so I thought, "To hell with it, let's give it a shot." I enjoyed what I was doing with Kerry [Packer], but I thought there was more.'

Evans came to the United States in 1983 and established Davud Evans Enterprises (complete with the odd spelling). In the late eighties Evans ran disgraced entrepreneur Christopher Skase's American Qintex Entertainment unit. In fact, Evans made the fateful call to place Qintex Entertainment, which owned Hollywood studio Metro-Goldwyn-Mayer, in receivership in 1989, a move that precipitated the collapse of Skase's empire. In 1992 he moved to London to work for British Sky Broadcasting (BSkyB), the pay television company that had been created two years earlier by the merger of Murdoch's Sky Television and British Satellite Broadcasting (fellow Irregular David Hill was the man who put BSkyB on the air). Two years later Evans landed in the United States as president and chief operating officer of News Corporation's Fox Television, overseeing activities including Fox Broadcasting Company, Fox Television Stations and Fox's FX cable channel.

'America was just bigger,' Evans says. 'You have the whole world at your feet and if you come up with a good idea in this market, your idea can be that much bigger. At the time I came here I felt like a very small fish in a huge bloody pond. It was a little unnerving. But I did have a desire to see how I would do in a world market. That certainly was more than just in the back of my mind. I felt I just didn't want to continue what I was doing in Australia for another 20 years. I didn't see the opportunities in Australia that existed over here.'

In July 1996 Evans became executive vice president of News Corporation in the United States and established the satellite pay television group Sky Entertainment Services Latin America. A year later he joined Tele-Communications International as president and chief executive officer. Evans then approached Hallmark Cards about creating a pay television channel and in 1999 was named president and chief executive of Hallmark Entertainment Networks. The company now has offices in Los Angeles, New York, London and Sydney, and its movies and television miniseries have won more than a hundred Emmy Awards, 13 Golden Globes and numerous other accolades. Hallmark Entertainment, as it is now known, owns a majority stake in Crown Media Holdings, which operates and distributes the Hallmark Channel in the United States. The Hallmark Channel has about 88 million subscribers worldwide and is available in roughly 120 countries.

'As things got more interesting here over the years, it just became more obvious that Los Angeles is the world headquarters for what I do,' Evans says. He has now been overseas for 21 years, all of it in the United States except for his two years in London with BSkyB. 'Hollywood — if you want to call it that — is the only place in the world that produces television that sells all over the world. If you want to be in the television business mainstream, this is where it is. For that reason, I stayed on and on and on and on. But I always had it in the back of my mind to return to Australia.'

For many Australian trailblazers in Hollywood, the relatively small number of Australians following in their footsteps seems odd. DirecTV's Hill, for one, believes he knows exactly how successful many of his former Australian workmates would perform.

'When I look at some of the guys I worked with in Australia — cameramen, directors, producers — they'd eat it. They would absolutely eat any competition in Britain or the States. I don't know whether there's something about us, whether there's something about our upbringing as Australians that makes us competitive.'

Hill came to the United States in 1993 to head News Corp's Fox Sports after the company won the broadcast rights to America's National Football League. After rising to the pinnacle of Australia's television production industry — he started Channel Nine's *Wide World of Sports* and headed its Olympic Games coverage, among many other events — he had worked in England before coming to Los Angeles. But while some fellow producers and cameramen in Australia decided to stay put, Hill wanted to see what his overseas competitors were made of.

'It always ticked me off that I would see other sports producers around the world and I'd figure I was just as good as them,' he recalls. 'I don't think it was a conscious desire at the time, but it must have been a huge motivating factor that I wanted to test myself against the best in the world to see how good I was. Or not, as the case may be. And I'm always interested in building things. I like start-ups. I wanted to put myself into someone else's environment and test myself. I don't think that was a conscious thought at the time, but certainly when I look back it obviously was there.'

So just why do those Australians who choose to take the risk of coming to the United States seem to do so well? The fact that they are Australian certainly helps, at least in terms of singling out an individual amid a sea of competitors, all jumping up and down, vying for attention. 'I'm just one of 1000 producers in the San Fernando Valley,' says Los Angeles–based Greg Coote. Being Australian is 'what makes me different'. Other Australians living and working in America have other, more complex explanations that have much to do with the kind of individuals who, in the first place, are willing to uproot their lives and try their hand in a foreign country.

'It's hard to generalise but I suspect they're very independent people,' says James Gorman. 'You come here with very little family history or connection to the place, with almost no network. Probably nobody in your family has ever spent any real time here. You're in really foreign territory.'

Bruce Stillman agrees: 'People who are motivated enough to come to a foreign country because of their career . . . it means you're a certain type of person. You're motivated, you're passionate about what you're doing. I came to CSHL because it was literally one of the top places in the world for the research I was doing. I think the same mentality applies in industry. You're looking for a certain type of person and that is a big selection in itself. It's independence, motivation, a passion for what you do.'

There's no doubt that moving overseas is traumatic. Giving up a job in Australia and leaving family and friends and established support networks — especially if there is no job to come to, as is the case with many younger people coming to the United States — is unquestionably difficult. Even the hardiest individual will be hard pressed to ignore the intermittent pangs for home when spying tiny jars of Vegemite on sale for more than US$5 or when, channel surfing late at night, the Australian Football League high-lights show appears. Indeed, the fact so many people are prepared to voluntarily step into unfamiliar territory and endure all that entails speaks volumes for the common character traits that link them, which include courage, determination, humour and ambition.

'I think it requires someone who's very comfortable being on their own and forging forward by themselves,' says Gorman. 'The Australians who come here to work do well — that's my experience. They consistently punch above their weight. They consistently do that. It's self-selection: you're getting people who are highly motivated, highly independent; who come here to succeed rather than do a tour of duty; who are prepared to take the consequences of that success, meaning they may not go back and that doesn't intimidate them; and who figure out how to work in American society.'

Settling in is crucial and expatriates agree Australians tend to follow one of two paths: they fight the culture in which they suddenly find themselves immersed, or they decide to work with it. That's not to say you won't find Australians gathering in places such as New York's Eight Mile Creek to eat fish and chips and watch the cricket via satellite television, but it is a delicate balancing act to retain your essential Australian character — not to mention accent — when surrounded by people and attitudes that are vastly different, even if the language is the same. Many Australians expect America to be very similar to home, and while in some ways it is, in countless others it is very much a foreign land. Hill believes Australians who have lived in the United States for any length of time develop a distinctive character, although he can't exactly define it. It has everything to do, he says, with that effort to fit in.

'I could never define why we're all alike, but we are,' he says. 'There are two types of Australians: there's the Aussie who is uncomfortable and can't wait to get back and wears his R. M. Williams boots on his head, and he says 'Mate' and 'How ya going?' with an accent so broad you can cut it with a knife. Then there is the Aussie who, chameleon-like, drifts into the culture of the country he or she lives in and makes the small number of adaptations necessary to fit into the society. And that kind, male and female — we all have a similar gene.'

Dow Chemical's Andrew Liveris agrees wholeheartedly with Hill's assessment that there are two essential types of Australians living in the United States. The Darwin-born chemical engineer believes Australians possess a unique ability to blend into different cultures. Liveris should know: while he came to live in the United States most recently in 1999, he and his family have been overseas for a total of two decades as a result of Dow Chemical postings in cities including Hong Kong and Bangkok.

'That first lot [those who cling to Australia], you see the casualties along the way: the people you've known over the years who have been overseas with you but who went back home,' Liveris says. 'I wouldn't call it homesickness. I'd call it being fairly blind to what the world brings. A lot of them want to go home because it's familiar. But the other type of Australian, those who blend in: it's pretty unique that there are that many Australians overseas — one million people — and the reason for it is, I think, Australians have a sense of adventure associated with their distance from the rest of the world, their physical distance. You won't find too many expatriates of other countries who blend in to that degree. They still retain their Australian-ness, their Australian identity; they are proud to be Australian and at the same time create synergy [within the companies they work for]. That differentiates the Australian.'

Ambition is another common character trait among Australians working overseas, particularly in a country like the United States, where there is such a high ceiling on careers. In fact, one of the appealing and somewhat comforting elements of coming to America for many senior executives is the knowledge that they are unlikely to have to move again. With the country boasting the head offices of so many companies, you can settle in the United States and work your way up through the ranks, or switch to another company in the same industry, without having to relocate any further.

'I think Australians with ambition, Australians who are driven — and that means a lot of people, certainly the ones who are overseas — they really can reach heights, reach responsibilities that are not available back home,' says Liveris. 'The American system seems to allow that regardless of where you are from.'

Liveris has been at the helm of Dow Chemical since November 2004, an appointment that was the culmination of a 28-year career with the company. Just 51 years old, he remembers at times feeling 'astonished' at how well he was doing within the company but quickly adds he believes 'overachievement is common amongst Australians over here'.

'Even within Dow I can name another half dozen Australians we have in our ranks,' Liveris says. 'You ask why? Why is Australia producing such a disproportionate number of overachievers? And you reach one conclusion: relatively, there are some attributes of Australians in a business institutional academic environment that are endearing and create the opportunity for success. I come down to this directness, this feet-on-the-ground down-to-earth-ness, this ease in fitting in to all sorts of environments. In the US in particular, I think. Americans really like people who blend in and accept their model, but they also applaud success. And back home the successful Australian hasn't been much applauded.

'It's changing, I know, and that's really great to see. There was a time when I would go back to Australia and I wouldn't say a word about what I was doing. I think the American model allows

Australians to overachieve and I think the competencies Australians have shine in the American model, because the driven Australians — the ones with ambition — put those skills to work very quickly. And let's not forget mateship. Australians have camaraderie. We're at ease socially, whether it be our legendary beer drinking or love of sports or the outdoors, or our fighting capabilities in wars . . . Australians are easy to like. It takes the best of Australia and gives the best of the US and that combination is amazing.'

Walk down Wall Street or assiduously read American financial newspapers and one thing will become apparent: a disproportionate number of senior executives within US companies are not American. There are no hard numbers on it, and while Americans obviously still dominate, executives from countries such as Australia and Britain, South Africa and Sweden are there in ratios completely outweighing their countries' populations. Many theories have been advanced for this development, most centring on the impact of globalisation and the realisation that domestic experience is no longer adequate when candidates are being considered for senior roles in companies that operate in tens of countries around the world.

'I think you're getting a very talented gene pool from these foreign countries that come into the US to work,' says Morgan Stanley's James Gorman. 'Just as Australians punch above their weight, I bet many countries reflect that. The fact that you're a foreigner, that you've lived and worked around the world, can't hurt you at all. But a heck of a lot of Americans have lived and worked around the world, so it's hardly unique. I think it's more a function of the gene pool and the talent pool that is there.'

It is certainly a change from just a decade or so ago. The relentless tide of globalisation has forced US multinationals to rethink the qualities they look for in executives, a turnaround from the days when managers from countries other than the United States, including Australia, seemed like aliens who had stumbled onto the wrong planet. A quick review of America's top companies delivers instant confirmation that times have changed. Brazilian Alain Belda heads aluminium giant Alcoa. Pharmaceutical group Schering-Plough is run by Pakistani-born Fred Hassan. The Indianapolis-based pharmaceutical giant Eli Lilly is headed by Moroccan-born Spaniard Sidney Taurel. When Australian Douglas Daft retired at the end of 2004, he was replaced at the helm of The Coca-Cola Company by an Irishman, Neville Isdell. An Egyptian, Louis Camilleri, replaced Australian Geoffrey Bible in 2002 when he retired from Altria Group. It does not always work out, though. Kellogg Company was headed by Cuban-born Carlos Gutierrez until in late 2004 he was named Commerce Secretary by President George W. Bush. In a surprise move, Kellogg passed over its New Zealand–born president and chief operating officer, David Mackay, as Gutierrez's replacement, instead naming American James Jenness to the position. However, if you are wondering if it is just the United States that is going global or whether it's an international trend, here's the most compelling evidence: last year Sony Corporation appointed the first non-Japanese chief executive officer in the company's 60-year history, Briton Sir Howard Stringer.

David Anstice, the president of pharmaceutical group Merck's human health division, has experienced first-hand the infusion of foreign talent into the American company.

'There was a period for quite a few years in the mid to late 1990s when at the management committee table I was running the US, Latin America, Canada; the guy running Europe was Norwegian; the guy that ran Medco was Swedish; the guy running our vaccine division was Egyptian with a medical degree from London,' Anstice says. 'Basically, we were running the operational side of the company and I often reflected on the diversity of backgrounds. All of them have been well educated outside the US. All of them have been very successful in the US. But the shared traits are that none of them had much time for bullshit: they were very straightforward, uncomplicated. And they all had a pretty good sense of humour. They didn't get hung up on ambition. I think a lot of Americans aren't always comfortable working with people below them; they're more comfortable looking up.'

Executive recruiters agree that the qualifications needed to run a major corporation today are vastly different from just a decade or two ago. Australia has some inherent advantages: the primary language is English, we have long exposure to American culture and we are necessarily international in outlook.

'The traits that I see are a willingness to take risks, to be more aggressive, more assertive,' Anstice says of Australian workers. 'I also see an interest in things globally, which is often lacking here. The US is so self-sufficient that people often aren't interested in what others have to say or do. I also see a practical side to most Australians, who just ask: what are we actually dealing with here? They're not getting lost in all the other stuff people get lost in. And they have a genuine affection for and interest in the people they work with, which I think is a real strength. Even in a big corporation, it's still people working there. You see many examples of businesses just ignoring problems. Australians just say, "It's got to be done. Let's not spend time debating it, let's do it." '

Peter Lowy has a theory about Australians' attractiveness to American multinationals that closely matches the opinion of Liveris. The second-born of Westfield Group founder Frank Lowy's three sons, Peter Lowy first came to the United States in 1980 to be an oil and gas analyst at Wall Street firm Furman Selz. Flick through the annual report of shopping centre operator Westfield Group, Westfield America's parent company, and you will find the man who gave Lowy that job — the firm's co-founder, Roy Furman — sitting on Westfield Group's board of directors. After a stint in London as a *'junior* junior in the merger acquisition business' at Credit Suisse First Boston, Lowy returned to Australia in 1983 and took over the operation of his family's finance-oriented Westfield

Trust. He went back to the United States with his wife and two children in 1990 for a single year on something of a fact-finding mission: 'to figure it out, see what's going on, and if we liked it, maybe make it two years and then come back'.

Fifteen years later Lowy shows no sign of moving. He is chief executive officer of Westfield America, which is now the country's second-biggest shopping mall owner, In fact, Westfield Group's US operation is now larger than its Australian business. Lowy believes Australians' ability to succeed in the American market is largely cultural — and special.

'I think Australians sit in a unique position,' he says. 'I was born in 1959. I grew up as a young kid in an Australia that was English — it was Australian, but it was English Australian. I went to Sydney Grammar, an English-style prep school, wore the caps and that sort of stuff. Australia then migrated, after the Vietnam War in the mid seventies, to a country that became more Americanised than Anglicised. What we're able to do now is come to the US, understand the culture, but understand the culture from a unique point of view; go to England and understand the culture from a unique point of view; go to Canada and understand the same thing; go to New Zealand and understand the same thing. In the English-speaking world, because we grew up as Australians, we have a unique perspective on the differences between each of those cultures and how to operate in them.

'You look at all the foreign executives in the US. I would argue that given the number of Australians and the size of the country they are probably, as a percentage, in much higher positions than would be expected. I would argue that's probably the same in the UK. How do so many Australians reach positions of such high authority in the UK and the US? Australia has melded those cultures. Especially in our business, it allows us to do the mall business in the US, the UK, Australia, New Zealand. We understand the culture of each of these countries. Even though they're different, we grew up with it all. We're embedded with all this stuff. I blame television. This is probably stupid, but I can still tell you things about television shows that were made here [in the US] or in the UK and shown in Australia when I was a kid.'

Saatchi & Saatchi's Bob Isherwood believes environments such as Australia foster tremendous creativity, a theory formed during the 17 years he worked in the United Kingdom from the late 1960s to the early 1980s. This view offers another perspective on just why Australians punch above their weight within the global business community, as do executives from many other, smaller English-speaking nations.

'I often wondered why in the UK the executives came from very good private education backgrounds and most of the creative people came from very poor backgrounds up north. I wondered why that was. I have a sense — and this may be just a crazy theory — that in a place like that, where there is huge depth of history, what happens is that the more you're exposed to what has gone before, the more inadequate you feel. So the better educated people start to think it has all been done. It's drummed into them.

'That's one of the things, to me, about Australia. You get this sense that it hasn't all been done. That anything new is possible in Australia. And I think there is probably a sense of that in America too. It is not an old country. Kevin [Roberts, the New Zealand–born global chief executive of Saatchi & Saatchi] has a great line: it's work in the new world, holiday in the old. We have an edge theory: we believe that change happens most at the edges of the planet rather than the major centres. Major centres are so encumbered by bureaucracy and infrastructure that change takes a long time to happen, whereas you look at countries like Australia, New Zealand, Latin America ... you see people with fresh ideas and points of view, and that's very useful for an ideas company like us.'

IBM's Doug Elix has lived in the United States since 1996 — his second stint in the country. He is quick to offer advice to those considering moving overseas.

'From a personal point of view, I have learnt that when you come to another country you have to set yourself up as if you intend to stay. If you try to set yourself up temporarily, you tend to get into a rut of moping and complaining and longing for the day you return. If you set yourself up as if you intend to stay, you make the experience all the better. I've noticed a lot of people say, "It's only two years, I won't get a big house and make myself comfortable," while others settle in. Those in the latter group end up enjoying themselves and learning.'

Elix also believes certain personalities are attracted to the challenge of moving to a country such as the United States, where significant barriers to entry exist. You won't find many Australians backpacking through the US and settling in to work behind a bar for a year — US working visa policies simply do not allow it. Under these circumstances, Elix's view is that the country attracts people who are 'achievement oriented' and willing to take risks, a theory supported in a tangible way by the country's ready availability of venture capital and support of entrepreneurship.

You might draw a broader analogy. 'There are no second acts in American lives,' wrote F. Scott Fitzgerald, only for society to prove that declaration resoundingly false. Executives in the United States who have fallen from grace are managing to resurrect their careers seemingly at will — from homemaking maven Martha Stewart bouncing back from a stint in prison with a reality television show and other lucrative deals, to developer Donald Trump brushing off flirtations with personal and corporate bankruptcy to be seen by millions of Americans as an avatar of business wisdom. The point is that the United States is a country that enthusiastically celebrates success and offers encouragement after failure. The tall poppy syndrome rarely rears its ugly face.

'Coming to the US ... it is a place where opportunity abounds for achievement-oriented people,' Elix says. 'It has something I call "systemic optimism": failure is accepted and trying again respected.'

Geoffrey Bible agrees. When he arrived in the United States for the first time in 1978, Bible did not sense corporate America's particularly entrepreneurial and dynamic spirit. Nearly three decades later, having run one of the world's biggest companies for eight years until his retirement in 2002, he does.

'I think the bankruptcy Chapter 7 and Chapter 11 rules here were ahead of their time and it's a shame other countries didn't practise the same thing for a long time,' Bible says, referring to the sections of United States Bankruptcy Code that provide shelter for financially troubled companies as they seek to restructure, refinance and work through their problems. 'Under our [Australian] rules, you went bankrupt and all the predators moved in and wiped you out and whoever gets in first gets the best flesh. Here you have a shot at putting it all back together again. It starts again, and you've seen that so many times with regenerations. The rules are really quite good. Looking down on failure here is not something that's part of the culture. Failure is seen as part of the journey. Some make it, some don't, and if you don't, that's okay: we've got rules that govern how we deal with it and you can start again. It's a very positive feature about America, but I wouldn't knock Australia for not having it and I think we're getting better.'

Putting it another way, Bible says, while he has 'always thought of Australians as get-up-and-go people — and that's one of their great characteristics — Americans are better'.

'We have the attitude that you have a go and if you fail, you maybe get a black eye. Here, it's step aside, start again. That's a good experience — not if you're a crook, but if it's a genuine attempt and it just goes wrong.'

Assessing the risks associated with uprooting your life to come to the United States, as against the comfort and familiarity of remaining in Australia, must be done on a purely personal basis.

However, Australians living and working in America have firm opinions about the benefits of moving, particularly for ambitious individuals eager to test themselves in the world's richest marketplace.

'There's no question that if you have the skills and competencies, Australia is a limited market in which to exercise those skills and competencies,' says Dow Chemical's Liveris. 'Whether you're in entertainment, in business or in the academic world, there's no question that the American market is the ultimate test. And for the past 100 years the American market has been seen as the market in which there is no limit to your ability to attain and achieve.

'So if you're driven, you're bound to be successful here. Whether you're an Andrew Bogut [the Australian athlete chosen in 2005 as the first-draft pick in the National Basketball Association] or a businessperson or an entertainer, you come to this stage because the Australian stage doesn't give you the scope. If you are driven, if you want to prove your credentials among the best in your field — unfortunately it's true for Australia and Canada and other small countries population-wise — you have to go elsewhere. Australians seem to do that much more readily and have a higher degree of success than most other countries.

'I think the percentages are higher probably because of the English language, common education systems in terms of what you learn and articulation skills. Remember the American propensity to reward the performance: is it the power of the presentation or is it the depth of the content? Form over substance? And if you can articulate and you have communication skills as well as knowledge of the content and substance, that's a pretty powerful combination in America. This is the great communication nation. Your ability to transmit your message, to motivate and engage people, is an incredible advantage. On top of that, I think, is the notion that Australians are very supportive of America.'

Yet this is not true for everyone. For all the Australians who come to the United States and are successful, many others quickly return home. Others stay and leave happily after a few years, their appetites satisfied. Individual experience seems to depend greatly on the level of expectation before arrival and the opportunities that present themselves once here, although it is arguable that the United States is a market where opportunities flow to those who are the most determined and hardest working. Given the common character traits of those who take the plunge and remain in the United States for several years, few top Australian executives are surprised by the success of their compatriots.

'I think it's kind of a personality trait of people who do take risks not to think about it until afterwards,' says Poppy King of the character of Australians attracted to the United States. 'Otherwise you feel a little inert; you can suffer from paralysis. It was only afterwards that I thought, "Wow. This is not my country." '

Col Allan, editor-in-chief of *The Daily Telegraph* (Sydney), 23 May 2001.

Merck & Co.'s David Anstice testifies during a product liability trial involving the withdrawn painkiller Vioxx, Atlantic City, NJ, 21 September 2005.

Geoffrey Bible, retiring chairman of Philip Morris Companies, in his New York office, 26 August 2002.
Newspix/Stuart Ramson

(BELOW) Hollywood-based Australian TV and film producer Greg Coote, Sydney, 21 January 2000.
Fairfax Photo Library/ Patrick Cummins

Atria Books publisher and executive vice president Judith Curr, September 2005.
© Rod Hernandez, Simon & Schuster

Doug Elix, senior vice president and group executive of sales and distribution of IBM, October 2003.
Courtesy of IBM

Hallmark Channel president and CEO David Evans, Los Angeles, 13 January 2005.
Getty Images/ Vince Bucci

James Gorman, president and COO of Morgan Stanley's individual investor group, 5 April 2005. © Fairfax Photos/Gabriele Charotte

David Hill, COO of DirecTV, at *The Australian*'s Media Forum, Melbourne, 26 September 2002. Newspix/Faith Nulley

Estée Lauder executive and cosmetics entrepreneur Poppy King, 2005.
© Akos

Andrew Liveris, president and CEO of The Dow Chemical Company, 2005.
Courtesy of The Dow Chemical Company

(LEFT) Westfield America CEO Peter Lowy, 2005.
© Greg Kinch Photography Inc.

(ABOVE) *Time* magazine's arts editor Belinda Luscombe, New York, 1 November 1998.
Getty Images/Time Life Pictures

S. G. Cowen managing director and global head of securitisation Greg Medcraft, 2005.
Courtesy of Société Générale

Lachlan Murdoch, News Corp's deputy COO, at the Bronx, NY, printing plant of the *New York Post*, April 2005.
Newspix/News Ltd

President and CEO of Ford Motor Company Jacques Nasser speaks at the North American International Auto Show, Detroit, 7 January 2001.
Getty Images/Jeff Kowalsky/AFP

(ABOVE) Film director Fred
Schepisi and wife Mary at
the première of *Empire Falls*,
Metropolitan Museum of
Art, New York, 9 May 2005.
Getty Images/Peter Kramer

(RIGHT) Cold Spring Harbor
Laboratory CEO Bruce
Stillman in his office, 2005.
© Bill Geddes, 2005

4 TWO CULTURES DIVIDED BY A COMMON LANGUAGE

Pamela Anderson. Admit it: you already have a mental picture. The Canadian-born pneumatic blonde actress was spotted at a football game wearing a t-shirt featuring the country's Labatt beer — the rest, as they say, is history. She became a model representing the beer company, moved to Los Angeles for a *Playboy* photo shoot, scored a role on the television situation comedy *Home Improvement* and then, in 1992, shot to mega-fame on the television show *Baywatch*, where she spent most of her time running in slow motion in a revealing red swimsuit. She has appeared in *Playboy* several times, and seemingly every other magazine aimed at titillating men. Given that everyone has seen her scantily clad, removing any possibility of surprise, perhaps the real shock would be to see Anderson fully clothed.

Not according to Wal-Mart Stores, Inc.

In 2004 New York–based publisher Atria Books, an imprint of Simon & Schuster, released Anderson's first novel, *Star*. It was described by trade magazine *Publishers Weekly* as a 'lighter-than-air debut' featuring a 'titular heroine [who] bears more than a passing resemblance to the author herself'. Suffice to say, it wasn't Tolstoy, but that hardly mattered. In the United States, books written by celebrities (or by ghost writers pretending to be celebrities) sell on the author's fame alone. Having Pamela Anderson on the dust jacket was sure to spur sales. And what a dust jacket *Star* featured: a nude Anderson, her breasts barely covered by a big pink star declaring the name of the book. If you were shopping at Wal-Mart, however, you would have seen something entirely different.

'We showed them this cover and they wouldn't take it because they said they'd get complaints,' recalls Judith Curr, executive vice president and publisher of Atria. 'They said, "It's too racy." '

To accommodate Wal-Mart, about one-quarter of *Star*'s initial 135 000 print run used a plain, hot pink cover featuring just Anderson's name and the novel's title — the publishing industry equivalent, perhaps, of a brown paper bag. Sneakily, Atria included a centrefold-style picture of Anderson on the inside of the dust jacket, but you had to remove it from the book to see it. Anderson's novel sold about 100 000 copies in hardcover, but at Wal-Mart, according to Curr: 'It didn't sell.'

For better or worse, in many ways Wal-Mart encapsulates many elements of American society. It was founded by Sam Walton in 1962, boasts more than 5200 Wal-Mart and Sam's Club stores around the globe, and is the world's biggest company in revenue terms: for the year to the end of January 2005 it recorded total sales of US$285.2 billion and booked a net profit of US$10.3 billion. Anyone who has shopped at Wal-Mart will understand the allure. Products are cheap and the range is mind-boggling, a combination which has given the company the financial clout equivalent to the thirty-third largest economy in the world — well ahead of most countries.

Yet Wal-Mart also reflects other, less positive elements of American society. It is constantly under fire for what critics allege are poor wages and working conditions, and a failure to provide comprehensive health benefits to employees. Less than one-third of its employees have any coverage under those insurance plans. Rightly or wrongly, Wal-Mart is seen as contributing to a business culture based on what are derisively dubbed 'McJobs' — low-paying, low-skill jobs and typically high worker turnover. It should be noted that McDonald's strenuously objects to the term, particularly when it appeared in *Merriam-Webster's Collegiate Dictionary* in 2003 with the definition 'low paying and dead-end work'. In an open letter to Merriam-Webster that was also released to the media, McDonald's chief executive officer at the time, Jim Cantalupo, said the inclusion of the word in the dictionary was 'a slap in the face to the 12 million men and women' who work in the restaurant industry.

However, Wal-Mart also often exemplifies another aspect of American society. With the company's roots in the southern Christian heartland — Wal-Mart's first store was in Rogers, Arkansas, and the company's headquarters is in neighbouring Bentonville — it does not hesitate to block the sale of products it believes offend 'family values', and this is where Atria ran into trouble with Anderson's book. Wal-Mart has been known to refuse to sell magazines such as *Cosmopolitan* and *Rolling Stone* because they featured covers it deemed 'too racy', and musicians have even changed album covers and song titles to appease the retailer. John Mellencamp airbrushed out an angel and a devil from one of his album covers so it could be sold through Wal-Mart, while Nirvana changed the name of the song 'Rape Me' to 'Waif Me' on its album, *In Utero*, whose back-cover artwork was also altered to appease the company. While some artists, such as Sheryl Crow, have refused to make such changes, it is understandable why others do: Wal-Mart is the biggest music retailer in the United States.

It is also among the country's largest booksellers. Atria ran into a problem similar to the Anderson book cover episode with an author few Australians have heard of: Zane. An African-American writer whose books appeal predominantly to black women, Zane writes hot-and-heavy romance novels. Curr holds up one of them, *Afterburn*, that Wal-Mart refused to sell. The cover features a beautiful black woman in a red dress being hugged by a shirtless black man, with Zane's name and the title running across the middle of the cover in a black band. At first glance it looks entirely acceptable. Curr points just below the black strip that bisects the cover: the man's hand is resting on the woman's behind. That was enough for Wal-Mart to act, even though significantly more scandalous content could be found within the book's pages.

'They're very prudish. Sexually prudish,' Curr says. 'This book, *Afterburn* — they ordered it and then didn't take it because the cover's too racy. They were afraid; they were worried about complaints. Then they got complaints that they didn't have it, so now they're stocking it. It's not the content of her books, it's the packaging they worry about.'

Catering to America's moral prudishness is just one part of the learning curve Curr has found herself on since moving to New York from Sydney in 1996. As editor-in-chief of Ballantine Books, then head of Pocket Books and now at the helm of Atria, she lives in Manhattan with her architect husband but travels all over the United States to tap the mood of her readers. She went to one of the country's hugely popular Nascar races and signed champion driver Jeff Gordon to write a memoir, and she attended a rodeo in Atlanta. Curr calls it 'looking at all the clues' of what makes people who buy Atria's books tick.

'I'm living in New York but dealing in the American marketplace. So the biggest mistake is thinking New York is like the rest of the United States. This year I've been to Atlanta, Miami, Raleigh, Durham, North Carolina. I go out into the suburbs and see the people who are hopefully going to read some of the books I publish and I see what they're up to.'

New York, frankly, is not like the rest of the United States. For Australians moving to the United States, it is even more important to understand that the United States is not like Australia. There's no doubt it is easier for Australians moving to America than it is for expatriates from many other countries: we share a language and similar technology, and we have been brought up with enough American television programs and movies to feel as though we are familiar with the culture. Yet as soon as you open your mouth you are made aware that you have entered a foreign land, both by the responses to your accent — usually you are marked down as British — and by people's struggles to understand you.

When Bob Isherwood first knew his American wife, their courtship had a few hiccups. Not long after their meeting, she went overseas and the pair communicated largely by email. With the benefit of hindsight, Isherwood says, he might have been better served to avoid that.

'She thought I was illiterate,' he says with a laugh. His emails contained Australian phrases and constructions, and the different use of language could make life difficult: 'For quite a long time, we'd have fallings-out over things that were cultural differences. We're two countries divided by a common language.'

Since assuming his current role at Saatchi and Saatchi in 1996, Isherwood has made a few unsuccessful attempts to work from Australia. After September 11 left his family temporarily homeless — they lived in Tribeca in downtown Manhattan, near the World Trade Center — they moved to Australia for a few months. Back in Sydney, Isherwood received a scare when his wife complained she was losing her hearing. A visit to a doctor prompted an appointment with a specialist and, after a battery of tests found nothing wrong, the following conversation:

'You're American?' the doctor asked.

'Yes,' Isherwood's wife replied.

'What about your husband?'

'Australian.'

'How long have you been here?'

'Three months.'

At this point the diagnosis suddenly became clear. The doctor said he had seen this phenomenon several times before.

'Your husband's just picking up more of an Australian accent, and sometimes Americans have trouble hearing because Australians tend to trail off at the end of our sentences,' the doctor said. Her hearing was perfect.

For Isherwood, the diagnosis was a relief and he now laughs about it. Yet it was also understandable: surrounded by fellow Australians again, he was unconsciously ending his sentences in that typically soft, trailing manner that forced his wife to strain her ears to understand him. Despite the absurdity of the episode, it is a reminder that sharing a language is no guarantee of clear communication. Many Australians report watching Americans' eyes glaze over during conversations — a reaction typically associated with being confronted by someone speaking a foreign language you don't understand. At some point many Australians have to remind Americans that they are, in fact, speaking English.

'It's a different language and there are different cultural touch points,' Curr says. 'Sometimes people just have no idea what you're talking about, particularly if you use Australian clichés. And sometimes there's no US equivalent. There are limitations on the language. There are not as many means to defuse situations using language, and that's probably why people are more diplomatic up front here. Every now and then I slip up.'

Many Australians seem to slip into a soft American accent unless speaking with another Australian, when their natural broad brogue returns. As Greg Coote puts it: 'We're in Rome, aren't we? If you want to get food, you better say "to-may-toe" occasionally.'

Television producer David Hill speaks with a distinct American accent most of the time, although he says he is never allowed to forget he is Australian. He advises friends on what Australian phrases to put to use in everyday life.

'It's not advertised that I'm a foreigner, but you're never allowed to forget it,' Hill says. 'It's something that's constantly brought up. You're reminded of it probably once a day.' As for the accent, Hill acquired an American twang for entirely professional reasons: when you are directing a live television broadcast, whether it's the National Football League's Super Bowl or a baseball game, there simply isn't room for confusion.

'I didn't have to change the way I work. I had to change the way I spoke,' the chief operating officer of DirecTV says. 'And there were two letters ... I was standing in a studio and I said, "Righto boys — we're going to rehearse halftime," and they all looked at me as if ...' Hill's voice trails off and he shakes his head. 'It's the "a" and the "r",' he explains. 'I've had to change, because in my business I have five seconds to tell someone something. If they've got to say "Beg your pardon?" or "What did you say?" then I haven't done my job well. So I have changed the way I speak.'

Hill consciously changed his accent after arriving in the United States in 1993. Since then, he says, his voice has simply altered to the point where he no longer even thinks about having to speak differently so Americans can understand him.

'It has just crept up over time. I think it's just living in this environment. I'll tell you something interesting, and I don't know when this happened, but I now don't hear Americans as having an accent. I hear Australians as having an accent and Brits as having an accent. When I watch television or listen to the news, Americans just don't have accents, and that's so odd. I hear myself speak, and I can hear my accent.'

When Peter Lowy arrived in the United States in 1990 with his family with a view to expanding the Westfield Group empire of his father, Frank Lowy, the company was a virtual unknown that owned just seven American shopping malls. Lowy was given a simple brief: to examine the market and, if possible, 'expand the business in the US'. Fifteen years later Westfield America has 67 shopping malls across the country and is the second largest mall operator in the United States. Its American assets outstrip those in Westfield's home base, Australia, and Peter Lowy's reputation is no longer a mystery. To listen to Westfield America's rivals in the shopping mall game, you would think the company is the toughest ever to lay a foundation stone.

Lowy rolls his eyes at the suggestion that Westfield America is anything other than a company that stoutly defends its interests. Business is business, after all. But he concedes that the company's negotiating tactics initially ruffled industry feathers. The different approach to negotiations was brought into stark relief for him early, since he began his working career on Wall Street with investment bank Furman Selz. He went back to Australia for a decade before returning to the United States.

'I understand the culture and the country,' Lowy says of America. 'The first thing is that real estate in the US has its own set of cultures as well: If you wanted to buy something worth ten dollars, in Australia you'd go and bid nine dollars. The seller would ask for eleven and you'd end up wherever you end up. In the US, if it's worth ten, they ask fifteen or twenty, and the buyer would bid five and then they haggle, they walk out, they walk in, you do everything you do, and you'd settle at ten. When we first came here, if it was worth ten we'd bid nine. The seller would go fifteen and expect to settle at twelve. We bid nine. Nine is nine. So I think the company got a reputation for being hard-nosed. You bid nine, it's nine.'

Most people have seen American movies or television shows where groups of male and female executives wearing expensive suits huddle around a boardroom table. Within hours, darkness has descended outside but the room remains brightly lit, Chinese food delivery cartons strewn across the table. They have all removed their jackets, the men's ties are askew, and the parties are haggling over every minute detail of a multi-billion-dollar deal. It usually ends as the sun rises, the negotiators collapsing after the marathon talks during which they were oblivious to the demands of time — to everything except the deal. It might be Hollywood's interpretation of what takes place in corporate America, but in fact it is sometimes not far removed from reality.

'The negotiation is part of the game here, whereas we want to get the negotiation over and get on with the job,' says Lowy, who knows all about multi-billion-dollar negotiations — Westfield America has struck deal after deal on its way to amassing an American shopping mall portfolio worth about $18 billion. 'The journey to the deal is as important as the deal here. And if you talk to any of the deal-makers, there is a culture here that no deal gets done unless you've spent all night arguing. Deals finish at three or four in the morning. They don't want it too easy. If you agree after an hour, they feel like they've left something on the table. A lot of deals fall apart because you're too tired, you're too emotionally involved and then everyone gets back together after a night's sleep and they do the deal.'

Although the relatively insulated American shopping mall industry is huge in numbers terms, it remains dominated by a handful of companies. Westfield America's competitors have simply adjusted to the way the company does business. Lowy notes that he has also picked up some habits in the United States and finds, when he regularly returns to Australia, that his 'attitude to business is so Americanised compared to everyone else in Australia that the cultural difference is now me'. Fundamentally, however, he simply believes there's 'nobody on the planet who is as upfront as Australians'.

'They [Americans] think you're obstinate and you dig in and you won't move, but it's just how you portray it. After you spend enough time doing business with people, they understand that Australians usually do what they say and say what they do.'

Other Australians have to tread more carefully, particularly those working within large, established, bureaucratic corporate cultures. Lowy has a big advantage in that Westfield America is a unit of an Australian company and he is undoubtedly its principal player in the United States, not to mention the fact he is Frank Lowy's son.

'For me, it wasn't as if I was the top student in uni or came out of law school as the top guy and then decided I'm going to America to test myself against the best there is. That was never part of it for me,' Lowy says. 'I look at it this way: I got really lucky. I was in the right place at the right time with the right economic factors, and the company was well equitised to take advantage of those factors, so I lucked out.'

For people like Doug Elix, dealing on an interpersonal level with employees of a huge company like IBM — the computing group has more than 300 000 staff worldwide — requires adjustments to be made.

'I think there's a tendency to incorrectly assume that it [the US] will be similar and it's quite the opposite,' says Elix. 'American culture is quite different from Australian culture. Just because we have McDonald's and we speak English doesn't mean we are the same. There are some significant cultural differences, and I think from a business point of view that is the first thing Australians who come here have to remember. There's only one of you. Don't fall into the trap of trying to convert America to you.'

One of the most noticeable features of corporate America also happens to be one of the most ridiculed — meetings. While companies in all countries rely heavily on the lack-of-work forum that meetings represent, America has raised it to an art form: the joke is they have meetings about whether to have meetings, then another meeting to decide whether the meetings about whether to have meetings came to a resolution. Then more meetings follow. Reasons for the preponderance of meetings vary, but — like many other aspects of American corporate culture — they seem to be a natural extension of big organisations dealing with multiple issues, usually involving large sums of money. While no one doubts the value of sitting down with colleagues to resolve issues, many Australians believe much more can be achieved in less time with fewer people around the table.

'Lots of meetings. Lots and lots of meetings,' Curr says. 'Maybe it's a product of size — when there are many more people involved, it takes longer to get things done because everybody has to come on board. Specifically, this industry [book publishing], as a creative industry, is about coercion and building enthusiasm and excitement and bringing everybody around to your point of view. Everybody wants to be included and because there are more people to include, sometimes it's just easier — and I don't want to sound like a dictator — to say, "No, this is what it's going to be. I don't care if you prefer that."'

Many Australians express frustration at a seeming unwillingness by Americans to engage them one on one, the context in which it would seem most likely that quick decisions could be made. Everyone likes to feel 'in the loop'.

'I'm not sure whether [people's need to be involved] is specifically American or has taken place elsewhere at the same time I've been here.' Curr was at Transworld Publishing in Australia for 17 years before coming to the United States in 1996. 'I think it has got a lot to do with the Internet, because everybody addresses everything about everybody in the universe, therefore inviting their participation and comment. And then you have to have meetings to sort that all out. When I was in Australia, email wasn't so prevalent. That could be a product of time rather than different cultures. Also, the more people are involved in a decision, the less people have to actually make it, in a funny way. The work style is different.'

One explanation for the desire to diffuse information among as many people in an organisation as possible is because, in the process, you are also diffusing responsibility. In many ways, that seems counterintuitive in a culture perceived to be as entrepreneurial as that of the United States: here is a country with the deepest venture capital pockets in the world, a fulcrum of innovation and creativity, and yet people are not willing to go out on a limb? Despite the headlines attracted by adventurous decision-makers such as News Corporation's Rupert Murdoch and Oracle Corporation's Larry Ellison, the wheels of the bulk of corporate America creak around thanks to the efforts of anonymous workers in grey flannel suits. Within large organisations — which is where expatriate Australians, particularly professionals, typically find employment — there are many fingers in every pie. Everyone fulfils a specific function, and it can often be difficult to identify a single individual who is driving an initiative.

'I had assumed, I think, I had this vision of particular New York businesspeople being very leading edge, very entrepreneurial and, as individuals, strong risk-takers,' says Ros Coffey, a human resources professional who is now senior vice president and chief adminis-trative officer of finance at investment bank Lehman Brothers. 'In fact, I found the opposite to be true. People ask permission a lot more than I expected them to. Some people would say it's a much more inclusive type of culture ... but sticking your neck out is maybe less likely; people are less prepared to take a personal risk. I find that very, very surprising.'

Coffey was working for Esso Australia when the company shifted its headquarters from Melbourne to Sydney. 'I couldn't possibly imagine moving that far away from home, so I went backpacking,' she says, laughing. After six months' backpacking around the world and 18 months of doing odd jobs in London, at the end of 1992 Coffey found herself working in the financial control group of an investment bank. Realising she had no desire to be an accountant, she then moved into the executive recruitment industry with Michael Page International. In October 1997 she was asked to open Michael Page's New York office, and she has been in the city ever since.

'There was no intention to come here — it was somewhat fortu-itous,' Coffey says at a coffee shop near Lehman Brothers' New York office on Times Square. 'I was the director of the financial services practice [at Michael Page in New York]. Lehman Brothers was one of the companies I worked with, and at the end of 2002 they asked me to come across and work in-house. I was the global chief admin-istrative officer for the finance division. About a month ago [in early 2005], I took on a different role, as global human resources director for finance, risk and corporate advisory.

'I don't think I envisaged a career overseas. I was always very career ambitious, so I'd always thought I'd do something decent, although I didn't ever imagine that I'd do it overseas. But you realise there are opportunities presented to you that may not be available in Australia. I couldn't do this, for example. It did sort of take on a life of its own, to be honest. I could never have thought I'd go to New York to open a business. I think it gives you a bit of a "have a go" attitude — you've got to give it a whirl. You also appreciate the enormity of what you're presented with and don't take it for granted.'

Having worked in both the United Kingdom and the United States, Coffey was also able to assess the differences between working in each market. The United Kingdom, of course, has for decades been a favoured destination for Australians, particularly young people, largely as a result of the availability of working visas. Coffey sometimes found it difficult to overcome British preconceptions.

'The view of Australia in some of those circles was, "You're Australian? Why aren't you working in a bar?" As an executive recruiter in London, she would nonetheless often be asked specifically if it was possible to find an Australian or New Zealander for a given job. 'People would say, "Here's a job I need to fill and if you can find me an Australian or a Kiwi, that would be fantastic." We have a reputation for being fast and decisive and for doing a good job. I thought I wouldn't have a problem adapting to New York. But it wasn't easy, probably because of the way Americans market themselves.'

If you accept the premise that only genuine truths become clichés, then you can understand why Americans generally have a reputation for self-promotion. There certainly seems to be a more general disposition in the United States towards the lauding of accomplishments, whether your own or those of others. And in a country with a population of almost 300 million people and sometimes thousands vying for a single job, the attitude seems to be that if you don't personally talk up your abilities, no one else is likely to do it for you. No one is likely to notice you if you don't push yourself forward.

'You have to learn how to really sell yourself,' says one-time lip-stick entrepreneur Poppy King. That can be difficult when you come from a country where big-noting your achievements is frowned on. Interestingly, however, while expatriates note that Americans tend to appear self-confident and in control, that does not necessarily mean they are comfortable speaking out in groups or putting themselves in situations where their skills might be publicly tested. King has found that while Australians have to rein in their natural inclination to tell it like it is, keeping a little of that habit is not necessarily a bad thing. It can, in fact, work in your favour.

'If you can learn how to use that kind of straightforwardness wisely, sometimes you can really disarm people. I'm someone who's never shy about holding my hand up and saying, "I don't understand, can you explain?" America is much more about the constant need to appear competent, whereas in Australia competence isn't measured by your talk; it is measured by your results. Ultimately, I think it comes down to results.'

David Anstice puts the same point slightly differently: he believes Americans, particularly men, are often simply 'full of bullshit'. Like any workplace, there are people who skate by on bluff and bluster, yet the highly decentralised nature of American corporations — where meetings are attended by many more people than actually need to be involved on a given issue — encourages individuals to make a noise if they want to be noticed. Many Australians say the people making the most noise fully expect not to actually be tested on whether what they are saying is true, largely because workmates are reluctant to put themselves out on a limb by challenging them.

'There's a sort of diffusion of responsibility that leads ultimately to a diffusion of accountability,' Anstice says. 'It's almost as though that's encouraged. I have reacted negatively from time to time to people's failure to step up and take responsibility.'

Anstice heads pharmaceutical giant Merck & Co's human health division, essentially the company's sales and marketing operations. That's a huge job: despite the negative impact from its voluntary withdrawal of popular painkiller Vioxx — and the lawsuits that resulted — Merck is expected to record revenues of about US$21 billion in 2005, down from US$22.94 billion in 2004. Anstice has worked for the company for 32 years and has operated from the company's global headquarters since 1988.

'I have found, and this is a broad generalisation, that American male professionals — not females — are more willing to bluff their way through things and, just frankly, to bullshit. And I think one thing Australians have is a good bullshit detector. I just find that white males, in particular, are full of bullshit sometimes and the less they know on something, the more opinionated they are. I find women do not exhibit that at all.

'What I do find is that the American professional women I work with are just terrific. Really very thoughtful about things; very broad-based in their assessments; always willing to listen and hear another point of view. They really seem to be motivated less by their own advancement and more by the merits of the case.'

Nevertheless Anstice did have to make his own adjustments when he came to work in the United States. Having worked for Merck in South Africa and managed its Australian operations, he was unprepared for the intellectual rigour of being at the company's head office. American companies might employ a lot of bullshitters, but they also employ a lot of incredibly smart people. On arriving at Merck's headquarters, then in Rahway, New Jersey, in 1988, Anstice faced a lot of challenges.

'My wife couldn't join me for the first six months and that was probably a good thing: I found the first six to nine months very grueling. The second issue is, because it was a staff job and you're supporting countries around the world, there's a lot of ambiguity in your role. You don't have specific line responsibility. The first six to nine months were very hard and I remember sometimes wondering whether I'd made the right decision.

'Then, at about month eleven, I got swung into the senior marketing job in the US and it was really the first senior-level appointment there. I guess some aspects of my skills suited me there, although equally I was not trained to do the work they asked me to do. But I did have a truly international perspective. I could work with multiple cultures and they saw I could do it at a practical level. What I found was there was a much higher level of professionalism than I had experienced in Australia and other parts of Merck. It was rewarding, but it was sort of like I was trained for the 400 metres and suddenly I was in a 1600-metre race. I figured I'd learn and adapt, which is what happened.'

He obviously adjusted: by 1994 he was president of the human health division for Europe then took responsibility for the same operation in the United States and Canada. In 1997 he assumed control of human health for the Americas, before ascending to the top divisional position on 1 January 2003.

'I can see where some of my cross-cultural experiences and skills and even patience are helpful,' Anstice says. 'I saw a lot of people here who weren't necessarily listeners to different points of view. People have seemed to be more interested in getting agreement based on what they thought at the beginning rather than listening and adapting. They were well informed up to a point, but not necessarily receptive. The adjustments were to the complexity of issues, the sheer volume and number, and the fact that there were so many people, including so many smart people.'

Ros Coffey also believes Australians' distinct character and penchant for direct talk can work in our favour. However, she agrees you have to use that skill within the peculiar US model, which requires people to say, 'I like the idea — but have you thought of doing it this way?' rather than, 'That's crap.' Many Australians say they have found themselves in hot water for being too blunt.

'I think you can turn it to your advantage,' Coffey says. 'Because a no-nonsense culture is something we are brought up with, we tend to see the answer and are prepared to kind of go for it. You have to be a little smart about how you do it. You can't be the bull in a china shop. But I've seen Australians more able to drive things. I see Aussies as less likely to say "Look at me" than "Look at my approach." They're also prepared to say, "This is the answer, let's push it through." They're able to get people together and get things done.'

Fred Schepisi didn't wait to be asked to come to the United States — he simply went to Hollywood. After making his name in Australia directing commercials and then the 1976 movie *The Devil's Playground*, it was 1978's *The Chant of Jimmie Blacksmith* that put the director on the map: it was nominated for 12 Australian Film Institute Awards and won three, and garnered a nomination for the prestigious Palme d'Or (Golden Palm) award for best film at the Cannes Film Festival.

Schepisi secured an agent in Los Angeles who began pitching the director's original screenplay 'Bittersweet Love'. Everything looked good at Twentieth Century Fox Film Corporation — until Schepisi received a taste of the movie-making business, Hollywood-style.

'As I was about to come over [to Los Angeles], Alan Ladd got removed from the Twentieth Century lot,' Schepisi says, referring to the then head of the studio. 'I waited two months. I heard a new studio head was coming in. He was keen to continue with the film, so I got on a plane and got over there, and by the time I got there he had been marched off the lot and Sherry Lansing was now in charge. I waited weeks to get a meeting with her — which I didn't understand at the time but I do now, given that kind of job — and finally I got to meet her and I said, "Look, you're a new broom here and you probably couldn't care less about what I've done, but I don't get paid unless I complete my next draft. So give me one of the oldest secretaries you have and an office. I'll finish the draft, you can read it and if you like it we'll do something. If you don't, we'll part without any acrimony.' I asked for one of the oldest secretaries because I knew she'd know more about what was going on than anybody else.'

Schepisi landed on his feet — in a way. His secretary quickly secured a great bungalow at the studio for him to work from, as well as parking and executive dining privileges. 'For two months,' he recalls, 'it was great.'

'Bittersweet Love' was never made. When it fell through, Schepisi 'had to get a job pretty quickly, otherwise I'd have to leave America and I was up for a film called "Raggedy Man".' That production was also problematic: the actress slated to be its star, Academy Award winner Sissy Spacek, was holding out on signing on for the lead role, and the studio wouldn't sign Schepisi until Spacek was on board. Despite assurances the directing job was his, he smelt a rat.

'My lawyer and my agent rang up and said, "There's a film called 'Barbarosa' — it's pay and play and you're an idiot if you don't do it."'

He made *Barbarosa* — it was released in 1982 — and it was a good decision. *Raggedy Man* duly came out with Spacek in the lead role, and the directing gig went to ... her husband, Jack Fisk. That's a battle Schepisi could not have won, and another lesson in the way Hollywood operates. So why engage the studios and their bizarre version of doing business in the first place?

'In Australia I had worked mostly with a great deal of my own money,' Schepisi says. 'I might have been running a successful commercials business, but I wouldn't keep doing that. So (a) I wanted to be paid; (b) I had this feeling, which was different from what I'd had before, that if I went over there and made some commercially successful films, I would make a name for myself, which would allow me to do the work I wanted to do; and (c) I wanted to test myself against the world. I don't mean I wanted to show off or anything, I just wanted to see what the differences were — how I'd stand up in the pressure cooker of international cinema making. I think what I found was it confirmed how solid my knowledge was and my talent was. You can make the mistake of overrating what you are and who you are, because there are some incredible moviemakers in America — you don't have to look too far to find out who they are. I guess what you want to know is if you can mix it with them.'

You could hardly call Schepisi's career that of someone enamoured with Hollywood. He splits his time between the United States and Australia, partly by virtue of the geographic locations of his seven children, but when in America he prefers to base himself in New York. And even after critical and commercial success with movies such as *Roxanne* with Steve Martin in 1987, *A Cry in the Dark* (released in Australia as *Evil Angels*) with Meryl Streep in 1988, *Six Degrees of Separation* in 1993, and last year's smash Home Box Office (HBO) pay television mini-series *Empire Falls* with Paul Newman, Schepisi steadfastly concentrates on making only the movies he wants to make. Part of that determination stems from his dislike of some aspects of the way Hollywood operates.

'I started in advertising in Australia, and I ran a commercials and documentary company for a long time as well. My two biggest shocks were that I found Hollywood was like dealing with account executives and brand managers and marketing managers, just on a broader scale and with larger amounts of money. I was really shocked to see that: the corporate aspect of it all. And I don't like the research process: the test screenings and things. I watched films get absolutely emasculated for all the wrong reasons. There was a tendency to turn a special film into something that would appeal to a broader audience.

'Somehow I minnowed around within the majors, within the mainstream, but got to do interesting films. There were still people around who did them. Alan Ladd and I ended up making probably four or five films together when he was at MGM and other places. You never knew in the end which of those films was going to make money. That was the path I took: I was always generally pretty aware that if you made — let's call them "interesting films" — and they didn't return high profits, you didn't get killed in the process if you showed promise and they could have broken out. If you set out to make very commercial films and they don't make money, you were basically dead.'

75

That's not to say Schepisi didn't make films slated for commercial success. He picked out the 1992 movie *Mr. Baseball* starring Tom Selleck and 1994's *IQ* with Tim Robbins and Meg Ryan as 'comedies which would seem to have been commercial decisions'.

'But the original intention on those was way better than the result that came out. If you do *Six Degrees* and *Evil Angels* ... if you do that, it's so curious — the structure and all of the process is so unusual in the normal Hollywood system — that people find it hard to screw around with them. If you do a romantic comedy or a straight-out comedy, people really think they know it and they try to make it in a really formulaic mold.'

Schepisi, 66, now has permanent residency status in the United States — he holds a green card. While he has spent most of the past two years in Melbourne, where he prefers to do the post-production work on his movies, he has no regrets about staying away from Los Angeles as much as possible.

'I lived in Hollywood for a while and I've a lot of friends in Hollywood. I like the weather and all that sort of stuff, but I couldn't stand that everything is about the business and it was very hard to get away from. And it was about the business *as* a business, not the art. If you're in New York, you're in every bit of humanity. That's where ideas come from. New York is also, in a way, one of the cultural centres of the world. You might gather that I love New York! I'm sure it would be easier if I was around a little bit in LA ... but I also don't see myself specifically as an American or Australian filmmaker. I see myself as someone who makes international cinema.'

5 STRAIGHT TALKING: NOBODY HERE DOES FRANK

Herbert Henry Dow left Ohio in the 1890s, a young chemist with little money but an interesting idea. Dow wanted to extract bromine — the only non-metallic element that is liquid under ordinary conditions — from brine, and he needed a natural source. In the small farming and lumber town of Midland, Michigan, he found what he was looking for.

Midland is 170 kilometres north-west of Detroit, America's motor city and the home of the Ford Motor Company, Daimler-Chrysler and General Motors Corporation. While Detroit was at the forefront of American industry at the start of the twentieth century, Midland was not far behind: the town had rich brine deposits and the Dow Chemical Company was founded in 1897. The company's initial products included bromine and bleach, but within 20 years it had dramatically expanded, becoming a major producer of agricultural chemicals, phenol and dyestuffs, and magnesium metal. In the 1930s Dow Chemical moved into the production of plastic resins — including polystyrene, which it began making in 1937 — and it became crucial to America's effort during World War II, as magnesium was used in fabricating lightweight parts for aeroplanes.

At the same time, Dow Chemical joined with Corning Glass Works to create Dow Corning, producing silicones for military and, later, civilian use. Both companies have continued to grow, and Midland's nickname today is 'Dow Town', which is much better than a nicknamed based on its other landmark, the 'Tridge', a three-way pedestrian bridge that spans the Tittabawassee and Chippewa rivers. Midland has a population of just 42 000 people, but it has bragging rights out of all proportion to this small base: Dow Chemical is the world's biggest producer of plastics (E.I. du Pont de Nemours and Company, better known as DuPont, is second), and since buying Union Carbide in 2001 it has also become a major player in the global petrochemical industry.

For a businessperson, moving from a foreign outpost to the global headquarters of a company is akin to an athlete representing his or her state being named to the national team. In US terms, it's a call-up to the major leagues. Yet while most people assume the headquarters of global companies are to be found in big population centres such as New York, Chicago and Los Angeles, many are in fact located in small regional centres. In a country that values its history, it should be no surprise that these corporations cling to their origins and resist the temptation to move to more geographically logical locations.

In late 1999 Andrew Liveris found himself in Midland, Michigan. It was a circuitous path to the world headquarters of the planet's biggest plastics group that began in Darwin, where Liveris was born 52 years ago. He is from a Greek immigrant family that arrived in Australia in the early 1900s and settled in Palmerston, which was renamed Darwin in 1911 in honour of the British naturalist Charles Darwin, originator of the theory of evolution. Liveris completed high school in Darwin before moving to Brisbane to study chemical engineering at the University of Queensland, where he graduated with first-class honours. Winning a university medal gave him several employment options, but Dow Chemical spoke his language.

'Young Australians, whether college graduates or even before going to university, want to go overseas,' says Liveris, sitting in New York's Four Seasons hotel. 'Usually to Europe or England, but I grew up with a fascination for America. Maybe I was a little contrarian at the time. But when I graduated Dow's recruiting line was, "If you join us we'll show you the world, we'll send you for training in America." The other companies I interviewed with, multinationals as well, were not as definitive as that. They were, "Well, come and work with us in Melbourne for five years," and there was no promise of that. In my case, it was a direct match between my desire to travel and work overseas and Dow's recruiting line.'

Liveris joined Dow in 1976. Three years later he was sent to Louisiana for training for two years before heading to Hong Kong, where he worked for another two years designing plants and facilities in China and Korea. In 1983 Dow Chemical posted him to Adelaide before sending him back to Hong Kong in 1985. That stint in Adelaide was the last time he worked in Australia. The Liveris family — by now he and wife Paula, who is from Broken Hill, had two children — then moved to Bangkok, where their third child was born. A three-year stint in America began in 1992 and ended when he was named president of Dow Chemical Pacific in Hong Kong in 1995. Then in 1999 Liveris got the call to return to the company's headquarters. In Midland.

'It is a tiny little town in the middle of nowhere in Michigan,' Liveris says, with obvious affection. 'It's a quintessential American community: good neighbourliness, great values, very religious. Heartland. You may not know this, but a lot of America's corporations were born in these places, and Dow never left. We operate in 179 countries; 40 per cent of the top 200 leaders of Dow are foreign citizens; five out of eight of the top executives are foreign citizens. Yet many of them live in the middle of Michigan. How's that for a dichotomy?'

Living in a place like Midland after global cities such as Hong Kong and Bangkok necessarily required some changes. Yet Liveris feels his earlier stints in the United States — training in Louisiana 25 years ago and the three years from 1992 to 1994 — allowed him to figure 'something out that was very important for Australians to be successful in the American model, and that is that the thing that endears Australians to Americans is the very thing that can get you into trouble'.

'Australians are casual to a fault, open to a fault, direct to a fault. And the very things that make you successful, I think — through my own studies and anecdotally — as an Australian in American corporations is they all carry this feature that is generic to Australians, and that is a "can do, roll up your sleeves, work with the common man, no hierarchy, comfortable with the shop floor, just do it" attitude. I think there is a real go-get-it attitude that doesn't tolerate bullshit very well, doesn't tolerate listening to the sound of your own voice ... and those characteristics can get you into trouble in America.

'They want politeness, they like to be liked and they have some degree of naivety. I saw it in the years we lived overseas — the American people tended to cluster together and be American. They took their model and transferred it around the world, whereas the Australians assimilated. There were no Australian compounds — you were friends with everybody. That attribute makes us blend in very easily, but at the same time we can frighten Americans by being direct and stating the obvious and wearing it on our sleeves. You have to gain a sense of American diplomacy. Some people call it politics, where you have to really know when to hold 'em and when to fold 'em. I learned that. Coming back to the US this last time I already had those skills, and our expectation was not to be Australian in the US but to run an American company globally and be part of their community.'

In a place like Midland, that means genuinely being a part of the community, especially when you are the top executive at the corporation that sustains the town. While middle America is highly religious and many Australian executives working in similar locations find themselves suddenly attending church services, Liveris says it 'isn't so much a need to go to church ... I think you know that Americans are very philanthropic and very charitable — so you join community boards. My wife volunteers for the hospital and raises money for sick children. You fit into the community.' Liveris is a member of the Midland advisory board of Comerica Bank and the board of trustees of the Herbert H. and Grace A. Dow Foundation. He is also a self-confessed sports nut, running, playing basketball and attending games of the Detroit Pistons, the National

Basketball Association team that won the championship in 2004 and last year lost in game seven of the NBA finals to the San Antonio Spurs.

In recent years, slipping quietly into a society such as Midland might have seemed more difficult for expatriates aware of the disproportionate impact the United States has on the rest of the world. It is one thing to be privately dismayed at your host country's politics or society — whether America's strong religiosity or the Bush Administration's 'war on terror' or its environmental record — but quite another to air those concerns. Even if opinion polls show a growing majority of Americans are concerned about the direction their country is heading, it does not represent a licence to criticise — as an expatriate you will likely be howled down.

'You don't threaten the American citizen and say, "You don't understand the world, you're arrogant,"' Liveris says. 'You live life according to their tune and I think our ability to adjust and be flexible while still remaining quintessential Australians typifies those Australians who have been successful overseas.'

It is not exactly about reaching a point where something 'clicks', although Australians who confess to being unable to adapt to the American way of doing business don't survive. Liveris believes his time overseas and exposure to multiple cultures and business environments shaped his work personality to a point where he was able to excel no matter where or with whom he was working.

'There was no "clicking" but more an evolution,' he says. 'I was astonished, and maybe this doesn't sound sincere but I'll say it, I kept being astonished at how well I was doing. For somebody from the antipodes in Hong Kong, a long way away from corporate headquarters, or in Bangkok or wherever I worked, I was doing well in the corporate leaders' eyes. I was doing what Dow wanted me to do and at the same time succeeding. I keep trying to figure that out — what created that difference. And I think I was concluding, I was evolving to the conclusion, that I was not threatening the American way. I was complementing it. I was adding to it. I was being synergistic. Australians have that hand-in-glove approach to America. I think that's what endears us to Americans. We don't slap them in the face; we actually hold their hand and show them a different way. I was noticing that I could work well in the American model but I could work well while retaining Australian attributes.'

In November 2004 Liveris was named president and chief executive officer of the Dow Chemical Company Limited, replacing the retiring William Stavropoulos. Aside from the personal satisfaction, there were other rewards: in 2004 Liveris was paid a total of US$3.66 million.

Being a chief executive officer necessarily requires a broad understanding of an entire business. Some might suggest chief executives know a little about a lot, but a lot about nothing. That may well be the nature of the job, given that it is more strategic than operational. At lower levels within American companies, however, you are expected to know everything about what you do. Australians believe American employees are significantly more specialised than those at home. This seems to be a result of the relative size of companies and workforces and the breadth of operations. Being a generalist might be an asset in Australia, but not in the United States.

'In Australia you can fix the photocopier. In New York people would look at you like you were crazy if you tried,' says Guy McKanna, who spent nearly three years as vice president of corporate affairs at investment bank Merrill Lynch & Company's world headquarters in New York. McKanna returned to Australia in 2003 and is now the head of Sydney corporate affairs for National Australia Bank. 'They [Americans] are too specialised and they're afraid to step outside their comfort zone, whereas we'll get in there and do it. We'll just do what has to be done.'

That broad practical knowledge and willingness to give things a go has advantages and disadvantages, of course. For job hunters in the United States, presenting yourself as anything other than an expert in a specific field creates problems in a market where companies look to fill particular niches with individuals who possess very particular skills. There seems to be little interest in individuals with an obvious capacity to learn a role, largely because so many people who are already experts in that role are available immediately.

'You specialise in one or two areas,' says Poppy King. 'I think often it can be confusing if you present yourself as a jack of all trades. They say, "What's your skill set?" As someone with a wide knowledge of all aspects of the cosmetics industry, she initially struggled to find her niche. 'In Australia you can do a little bit of this, a little bit of that. I've found it very different here. It wasn't enough to say I had my own business. I had to say, "This is my skill set: I'm very good at x, y and z." There's not a lot of "go with the flow", that's for sure. You've got to kind of leave your home experience at home.

'The first year was very difficult. I think it took me the first year to work out that having talent and being effective … one does not necessarily denote the other. I think that year was very much about focusing on how to be effective. I've been here two and a bit years now, and the last eight months I've just really flourished. I can feel it and other people in the company can feel it. I've started to really hit my stride now and am really going in the right direction, and although I see being in New York for the foreseeable future, I really view this in the same way I view school — almost in terms of semesters. I'm interested in getting results in the short term and seeing what type of picture that ends up painting in the long term.'

The other adjustment King had to make was to the pace of work, notably in New York. 'The whole city is going faster. I don't think you work harder or more, just faster.'

When the editor-in-chief of the *New York Post*, Col Allan, talks of people working non-stop for ten months of the year and then holidaying for two — while still in intermittent contact via mobile telephone and email — he is not kidding. 'I think people are very productive here,' Allan says. 'I know a lot of people who work outrageously hard. They do in ten months what a lot of other people in other places do in a year and a half.'

Many Australians are shocked at the way work consumes American lives: annual leave may total just two weeks a year, and you become entitled to that only after working for a year. Breakfast meetings are standard, as are working lunches and drinks or dinner after work. Atria Books' Judith Curr gained weight when she first began working in New York and altered her schedule accordingly. It should be noted that she is now slim by any measure.

'In Sydney, you'd have a lunch meeting every couple of weeks, maybe once a week. Here it's every day,' Curr says. 'Now that I'm established, I have lunch only four days a week. I save one to go to the gym.'

The bottom line is that major organisations do not regard time away from the office as sacrosanct. Particularly in a city like New York, your personal life takes a back seat to work, which takes precedence over basically everything else.

'You need all your creative energy here — your life is an annex to your career,' says *Time* magazine's Belinda Luscombe. 'I have my job and my kids and that's it. That's 1000 per cent of my life. When I go back to Australia I'm incredibly jealous. In Australia we would work and then we would go and have a drink, and we would not be working. But when we were working, we were working. Here, the lines are very blurred. One reason is because you only ever get stuff through who you meet, otherwise no one ever notices you. The system by which you enter employment is too overwhelming and too Byzantine — its job is to weed out, not to bring in. It's not just that in Sydney you have all the smartest people applying at *The Sydney Morning Herald* or the ABC or whatever. Here you have the smartest people from 50 states and other countries. The corollary is people come into your office all the time just to have a chat. I learned that that's actually part of the work. You chat and you build a bond so that when you have to do something that's difficult, you can rely on that bond. That's how, as far as I can tell, things get done.'

When things go wrong, of course, the diffusion of information and the subsequent diffusion of responsibility can make identifying and fixing issues difficult. Luscombe works within the American magazine industry's unusual structure, which clearly delineates between reporters and writers: reporters do the legwork on stories, conducting interviews and doing research; writers, in *Time*'s case typically based in New York, take reporters' notes and fashion the story. In Australia, journalists typically both report and write stories. While it seems odd that *Time* stories are written by someone who has not done the first-hand reporting on the issue, the system is standard among US national magazines and allows information from multiple reporting sources to be objectively pulled together by one individual. But it also requires editors such as Luscombe to deal with several individuals on each story, which means tackling multiple egos.

'I had to be much, much more polite, much more courteous and cordial and a lot less frank,' she says of when she started as an editor. 'On the one hand, people liked the frankness, because nobody does frank. People are much gentler here in their treatment of each other. So in some ways the frankness helps, but only up to a point. I can say things to Australian colleagues here that would shock Americans. There is a lot more consulting here, a lot more working together. I think a lot of this is because there's a lot more money at stake in whatever you do in this country, and whenever that's true there's a lot more arse covering. You can't point the finger at one person. You say, "Mistakes were made." You can't say, "Belinda fucked up." You say, "Mistakes were made." That's a big phrase used around here. Or there was a systemic failure.'

Saatchi & Saatchi creative director Bob Isherwood describes the US business climate as 'ultra-conservative'. 'And that's partly because the sums of money involved are so large that people are risk-averse and it's about surviving — without having your head chopped off because something goes wrong,' Isherwood says. 'It's amazingly litigious. You're not allowed to ask someone their age or all kinds of things that for Australians would be considered normal. It's quite a culture shock.'

For the past four years, Los Angeles–based Coote/Hayes Productions has been a partner in ANYTIME, a video-on-demand company it formed with Macquarie Bank and Singapore-based YTC Corporation. Video-on-demand allows television viewers to watch movies whenever they want simply by pushing a button on their remote control — the film is sent to the home via satellite or cable, can be paused, rewound or fast-forwarded, and may be watched for a given rental period before expiration.

To get ANYTIME up and running, the company needed to bring major Hollywood studios on board to supply their product. The company has signed Universal Pictures, Twentieth Century Fox, Sony Pictures Television International, and Warner Bros International Television Distribution to supply deals for Asia and the Pacific Rim, and its service is already being distributed by junior telecommunications player TransACT to its pay television subscribers in and around Canberra. For people living in a city like New York, video-on-demand has been available for years through pay television operators including Time Warner — you can even watch your favourite television programs on demand, as well as pause and rewind live television with the use of a digital video recorder set-top box.

Yet for all the exciting technology involved in creating an on-demand business and the lucrative rewards that the industry promises, you have to feel for Coote/Hayes Productions' Greg Coote. That's because cutting a deal involving multiple Hollywood studios means dealing with multiple Hollywood lawyers, whose desire to be involved in every little aspect of every deal is mirrored across corporate America.

'Americans like to do business fast but it's endlessly overcomplicated by the law,' Coote says. 'I don't think there's any trust in any way, shape or form. I talked to someone at a studio the other day and then got a call from a lawyer at the studio: "You know, you really shouldn't do that without me." Business has almost ground to a halt as it is.'

During negotiations with Fox, Warner, Sony and Universal, Coote dealt with eight lawyers. Meetings degenerated into farce when none of the principals were prepared to talk about aspects of the deal without first consulting with their lawyers, largely for fear of breaching federal law. 'None of them talk to each other because of the Antitrust Act. The board meetings are hilarious because no one can talk to each other.'

Given events of recent years, such as the collapse of Enron Corporation and the troubles of Tyco International, WorldCom and others, it's no wonder American companies engage lawyers at virtually every stage of the deal-making process. Yet it again points to a corporate culture that is by its nature more cautious and less nimble. Some Australians dispute that characterisation, however.

James Gorman is among a handful of Morgan Stanley's very top executives, and an unabashed admirer of the American corporate model and its results. 'I stand back and look at the macro performance and there's more innovation that comes out of the United States than anywhere else in the world. That speaks to a business culture that is very dynamic and decision-oriented and prepared to take risks and put capital behind that risk. Australia would be hard pressed to claim that it is more innovative or decision-oriented or risk-oriented than the United States. It's certainly comparable in many sectors, but the US is not a bureaucratic country.'

Gorman worked briefly in Melbourne before coming to the United States in 1985 to undertake a Master's in Business Administration at New York's Columbia Business School. He believes the corporate cultures in Australia and the United States are not altogether different, at least in the financial services sector, partly because so many executives have worked in multiple locations. Many work at the Australian operations of major Wall Street investment banks — the head of Merrill Lynch's Australian trading business, Dan Ritchie, worked in New York for years — and, says Gorman, they 'don't behave or think very differently from the way we do in New York'.

'It's more intense, certainly, in New York than it is anywhere in the US. It's more competitive, more driven. That's something you would not find anywhere else, whether it be Chicago or Sydney or Melbourne. But they are very sophisticated cultures [in Australia]. The financial markets are very sophisticated ... so it's certainly not a backwater in any regard. It's another sophisticated international community; it's just not the same as New York. But nothing is.

'From where I sit, I'm not focused at all on whether something in the corporate world is Australian or not. It's more, "Who is the best practice operator? What do they do well?" Look at Macquarie Bank. Macquarie is an Australian bank that has done a phenomenal job. They're world class — they just happen to be headquartered in Sydney. I don't think of companies in terms of whether they're Australian or not, and I certainly don't compare us or anybody else in the US to Australian companies any more than I compare them to British or German or French or Japanese or Korean or a host of other countries.'

Gorman, who is seen as a potential future chief executive officer of investment bank Morgan Stanley, currently valued at US$61 billion, believes Americans can be just as straight-shooting as their Australian counterparts. Anyone who has walked the streets of New York, ridden on a subway or ordered at a deli knows he has a point: people often tell you exactly what is on their mind, for better or worse.

'I think that's one of those myths that people want to believe: the good Aussie straight talker,' he says. 'I mean, I've been in a lot of

meetings in Australia that are, frankly, very frustrating. I think, particularly in New York City, Americans can be very in your face and
tell you what they think.'

Bruce Stillman confesses he is 'fairly blunt and I'm constantly
told, "You can't do that".' But the CSHL chief executive also admits
he did not plan for a position requiring a great deal of diplomacy. 'I
didn't go into science or medical research to be an administrator or
to run a facility like this,' Stillman says. 'That's very different from
someone who really aspires to run a company. I never had a
thought of wanting to be president of a research institution — it
just kind of happened. My real interest is in doing science.'

However, like Gorman, Stillman believes the differences between
Australian and American culture are not that great. One of the
things that struck him when he first arrived at the Cold Spring
Harbor Laboratory to undertake a two-year post-doctoral stint in
1979 was how similar Australian and American cultures actually
were. Twenty-six years later Stillman is still living in Cold Spring.

'It's got even more homogenous now with television and films
and such. The one thing that struck me was that Australians tend to
have the right mixture between British humour and American get-
up-and-go and materialism. Americans have this "can do" type attitude. Australians have that and yet we have, I think, a better sense of
humour.'

Greg Medcraft arrived in the New York in 1999 to become the
US head of securitisation for Société Générale's investment
banking arm, S. G. Cowen. After working in Paris for the French
bank at the end of the 1980s, before returning to Australia for a
decade, he helped establish the firm's European and Australian
securitisation operations and was regarded as one of the world's
foremost players in the emerging industry. For Medcraft there was
one cardinal rule about working in the United States.

'One thing that you don't do is talk about how we did things in Australia,' he says with a laugh. 'I learnt that very quickly.'

Six years later Medcraft has no need to talk of his days in Australia. He co-founded the industry's professional body, The American Securitization Forum, and recently assumed a three-year term as chairman of the group after three years as its deputy chairman. The ASF boasts more than 100 members — including every major investment bank and corporation involved in the securitisation industry — and while Medcraft describes its evolution as 'very satisfying', it has served a handy dual purpose. 'It's also been good on the commercial side because it's allowed me to become quite well known. It's all about networking. It's about networking and proving yourself. Networking is really important.'

There are relatively strong Australian networks in the United States, assisted by local consular arms of the Australian government and organisations such as the American Australian Association, which was founded in 1948 and boasts associate patrons including News Corporation chairman and CEO Rupert Murdoch, former Coca-Cola boss Doug Daft, and former World Bank president James Wolfensohn. However, there is nothing approaching the Australian presence that has existed in the United Kingdom for decades, and expatriates in the US have been working hard to establish social and professional ties. Medcraft and other top executives work with an organisation created by the Australian Consulate General in New York, Advance — Australian Professionals in America, mentoring younger professionals and participating in social functions.

'I think it's more courageous to move to New York than to move to London,' says Medcraft. 'It's a much more worn path to London than New York. There's probably something to be said for the view that those who come to New York are a bit more gutsy than those who go to London. New York is a pretty tough place. There's no support. The more Australians who come, the better and stronger the network will be. I think it's becoming easier for Australians to come.'

Geoffrey Bible left Australia at the age of 21. Trained as a chartered accountant, he worked for the United Nations Relief and Works Agency for Palestine Refugees, Esso and the UN's International Labour Organization in Switzerland before joining tobacco and food giant Philip Morris in 1968. A decade later he was in the United States with the company; by 1995 he was the chairman and chief executive of one of the world's biggest corporations. Bible says he never thought of working in America as a young man — Europe was the traditional destination for ambitious professionals. Today his choice would be different.

'If I had to make that decision knowing what I know now, I'd find it difficult but I would plump for America,' he says. 'Of course, the work ethic here is much more similar to that in Australia. I think Australians can work hard — not that they all do, but they can. I think most Australians would want to come here and then go back to Australia, and they'd learn more here that would be applicable in Australia than they'd learn in Europe.'

National Australia Bank's Guy McKanna puts the choice more bluntly: 'While a lot of Australians go to London, they're just missing the point. New York is the modern place to be.' That is the kind of straight talking Australians are known for.

IBM's Doug Elix reiterates that our national character equips us with pluses and minuses when it comes to working in the US. It's all about working within the American corporate culture.

'Australians are more down to earth. They get to the root of a problem much more quickly, which enables them to solve it and move on. That's a plus,' Elix says. 'On the other hand, it can be a minus because Americans can see that as being overly aggressive and almost rude. There's a lot more process around how things are done here. Again, you have to be careful before saying that's a waste — there is a reason for it. It does introduce discipline and a way of getting things done more thoroughly. You just have to be more thorough.'

As Estée Lauder's Poppy King puts it: 'I don't think there's any point coming to something new and always comparing it with what you did at home. But I still very, very much consider myself Australian, and I don't think I'll ever consider myself anything other than Australian.'

6 THE BURDENS OF INTEGRATION

Judith Curr and Ken Kennedy got home late on Saturday, 2 March 1996. It was the night of the annual Sydney Gay and Lesbian Mardi Gras, an excuse for celebration not just among the parade's 5000 participants and the estimated 650 000 who lined Oxford Street to watch it that year. It had already become one of those nights when everyone in Sydney seemed to feel obliged to have a night out, and Curr and Kennedy had done just that.

They were entitled to sleep in. As part of the team that in 1981 founded publishing house Transworld, the Australian subsidiary of Bantam Doubleday Dell, Curr had for a decade been Transworld's executive director and publisher, making her one of the Australian book industry's top executives. Kennedy, her partner of 11 years, worked multiple jobs: he was a partner in an architecture practice, Quadrant Design; he edited the art, architecture and design magazine *Monument*; and he taught at the University of Technology Sydney and the Design Centre Enmore. Their sleep was about to be rudely interrupted.

The telephone rang in the early hours of the night. The call was for Curr: after several only half-serious pitches over the years to lure her to the United States, this one was for real. She was offered the position of senior vice president and publisher of Ballantine Books, an imprint of book giant Random House, in New York City.

'It was literally the middle of the night,' Kennedy remembers. 'The Americans called — they got the times mixed up — and they said to Judith, "We'd like you to come". We woke up later that day wondering if it was a dream.'

It wasn't. The couple had just two months to pack up their lives and move to the United States, a process further complicated by the fact they weren't married. In the middle of all the negotiations with lawyers about work visas, the decision was made: not only would they resolve their professional lives and pack up their house, but they would also be married before setting foot in America. Given the gravity of the decision to move to the United States together, it seemed only natural.

'It was more, I think, "We're making a big decision and let's go to Manhattan married",' Kennedy says. 'And there was a slight worry from the lawyers of Judith's company that coming here and not being married might make things a little difficult for me.' Not that having a marriage certificate necessarily solved that problem in itself. Kennedy found that Americans often remained confused because of their different last names. 'They would ask if we were married — and how could we be because our names are different? In the end I used to just carry around our marriage certificate.'

For Curr, the process was comparatively simple: although there were legal issues between the companies, basically she left Transworld and began work at Ballantine. For Kennedy, there was much more to be done. He had to resign from his architectural firm, and leave his teaching and magazine work behind.

'I was writing, teaching and practising, and it was a good balance,' Kennedy says. 'I just resigned [from Quadrant] ... My partner was concerned because we were at a stage where we'd developed the practice over 15 or so years, and I didn't want to leave him in the lurch. I had about six or seven commissions at the time, and I think he took over three and I farmed the rest out to friends.'

Kennedy understood the lure of working overseas. He had lived and worked in London for five years in the early 1980s. He was on a short return visit to Sydney in 1985 when he met Curr — and the rest, as they say, is history. But while others seemed to view with some concern his decision to sacrifice his career in Australia to come to New York, Kennedy insists it 'wasn't such a big decision for me in the end'.

'We talked about it and I thought it would be a great opportunity for her to work in another city, as I'd found in London. I was happy to drop everything and seek work in New York as well. Once I told other people, they seemed to be more concerned than I was.'

The biggest problem for Kennedy was the practical one that partners of people coming to the United States to work have historically encountered: he did not have a work visa. Curr came to America on an H1-B visa, which is typically issued to foreign professionals after their US employer petitions immigration authorities on their behalf. The applicant is described as filling a 'specialty occupation' for which an American worker could not be found, which usually disqualifies lower-level local employees. While it allows the primary visa holder to live and work in the United States and permits the visa holder's partner to live in America, it does not allow the partner to work. If you have been engaged in a fulfilling career in Australia, suddenly finding yourself in a foreign country and unable to work can be jarring. Many Australians talk of partners who become listless and fall into something of a malaise, struggling to adapt to days that suddenly need to be filled with activities other than work.

In many ways, Kennedy was fortunate. While he did not have a work visa for his first year in the US, Curr was able to support them both and he set himself the task of finding a place for them to live. After a few months of looking, they decided to buy an apartment on Manhattan's East Side, not far from the headquarters of the United Nations.

'Ken couldn't work for the first year, but we were lucky in that we were able to buy a small apartment in New York before it had its big boom,' Curr says. 'And because Ken's an architect, he completely renovated the apartment and it gave him two things: an opportunity to work here without working here; and, in the end, he had some New York work he could put in his portfolio.'

Kennedy found that the more he studied the New York property market, the more 'it became obvious that the market was very good for buying'. As for the renovation, he decided to 'turn it into a chance to show people what I could do'.

'I was fortunate that it [the completed project] was published in a couple of books, and that enabled me to get some commissions.' That publicity formed the foundation of his new architecture practice. 'It was basically word of mouth.'

The process of finding, redesigning and renovating their apartment took Kennedy past the point when he received authorisation to work. Using the couple's property as a real-life résumé, he has been able to build up a practice in New York. The few years they originally planned to live in the city has turned into nine years and counting. A big decision point came after German group Bertelsmann AG bought Random House in 1998. Curr and Kennedy received their permanent residency — that is, their green cards — in 1999, and Curr then left Ballantine to become president and publisher of Pocket Books, an imprint of Simon & Schuster. That role has morphed into her current position as executive vice president and publisher of Atria Books.

'We came with the notion of being here maybe three or five years,' Kennedy recalls. 'The decision [for Curr] to leave Ballantine was made a lot easier because once we had the green cards, we were free agents. At that stage I was starting to get a few commissions and could see that I could work here. My time in London made me realise that it wasn't a case of the poor hick antipodean Australian designers — we're just as proficient as anyone else. But there was no obvious decision to go and show the New Yorkers what I'm made of. I was fairly confident in my abilities without having to prove anything to the world.

'I've been able to establish a small practice just working on my own. As I develop new work, it then starts to bring Manhattan-based clients who have other work,' Kennedy says. 'I did a loft conversion for some people and they now want to build a house in Mexico; I did some work for some New Yorkers who now want to do some renovations to their house on Long Island.'

Everything has worked out for Curr and Kennedy. Aside from the Manhattan apartment, they own a property on Long Island, east of Manhattan, near the beaches and the Hamptons, and have fashioned a lifestyle that would be envied by many. Still, Sydney has a lasting allure and the challenge will be to fashion a life that incorporates the best of both countries.

'I think we'll certainly go back but I suppose, because we enjoy it here, we'd still like to keep some vestige of a life here,' Kennedy says. 'In the next five years we'd like to work out a way, if we can, to be in both places. Eventually we'd like to spend more time in Sydney, which I suppose eventually would be somewhere we'd love to live.

'The lure of Sydney is the climate. You do just sometimes get a little sick of the weather in January and February here. It's very much a New York proposition for those who are lucky enough to be able to do it: to have an apartment in the city and a house outside. The last three years of having the house [on Long Island] have made the city much more user-friendly, I suppose. But we're very lucky to be able to do that.'

Not everyone is so fortunate. Television producer Greg Coote's marriage ended shortly after his 1986 appointment to run the worldwide marketing group for Columbia Pictures, which required him to move from Sydney to Los Angeles. Coote, who in 1988 married an American and has two teenage children, initially came to Los Angeles alone.

'We'd split up when I left Australia and then she came and the kids came and it was okay but it just didn't work out,' Coote says of his first family. 'The marriage was falling apart, and at some point you can't put Humpty back together again. I never knew how long I thought I'd be here. I still don't know. I always feel like I'm on a business trip when I'm here, but I don't see myself going back to Sydney either. My dear old dad said, "Life is not a practice swing," and I just don't want to go on playing the same old tune. I love Australia and I love family and friends and I really enjoy myself when I do go down there, so I don't feel like I'm not there. But this a bigger ballpark, you know? It's hard to do it out of Australia. For me, it's a world stage, simple as that. And just because you're not living there [in Australia] doesn't mean you're not there mentally. I have a huge bias towards Australia — it's ridiculous.'

For couples who arrive together in the United States, life can be tough. That's not to underrate following a spouse or partner to the United States; tourists pay thousands of dollars to find themselves in cities like New York and Los Angeles with time on their hands. The problem for many professional men and women is suddenly finding themselves under- or unemployed, leaving careers that have been rocketing along the highway suddenly stalled on the shoulder of the road. With flat tyres.

'You can only go to so many museums, you can only do so much shopping,' says Kay Binnie, the wife of S. G. Cowen's Greg Medcraft. The couple came to live in New York in 1999. 'It's difficult, particularly if you don't have kids — and we didn't at that stage — because children kind of bind you into the community. And if you've been in a job and you come across without one, it's quite difficult to re-establish those ties. I really didn't manage to fill the void.'

The partners of many Australians living in the United States find themselves looking to each other for support. In New York, for example, a group of women in 1999 gathered to discuss the dilemma: the result was Australian Women in New York, which now boasts more than 200 members who gather for a variety of activities that provide social interaction. While the bulk of its members are in New York, women also come in from Connecticut and New Jersey for monthly meetings at the Australian Consulate General in New York — for its 'Mums and Bubs' group and for social outings.

For many Australians, however, part of the allure of being in the United States is to meet and socialise with Americans. Without a child to facilitate meeting other parents or a job within an American workplace, that can be all but impossible. And when your partner comes home every day, seemingly fulfilled with his or her career and content in the decision to leave Australia, family and friends behind, it can be difficult to cope.

Medcraft arrived in the United States in early 1999 while Binnie stayed on in Sydney, having only recently taken a new job in marketing and communications with management consulting group Accenture. With a Master's in Commerce, she hoped for a transfer within the company to a position in New York, which would have been an ideal outcome.

'For reasons beyond my control — a change of management — it was put on hold,' Binnie says. 'Then I was able to find a job in New York but the visa thing at that stage was very difficult. I was in the process of negotiating over the job and realised that if I couldn't do it fast enough, the visas were going to run out. It was so frustrating. That was during the dotcom boom and all the visas were gone by the time I tried to get one. Six months later, when they began issuing visas again, they were taking four months to process and the dotcom boom had ended.'

Without a work visa or a job, Binnie had almost two years of unemployment in New York. It might sound like a nice city to while away some spare time: after all, it is home to the Metropolitan Museum of Art, the Museum of Modern Art, the Guggenheim and countless other attractions. Yet it just left Binnie frustrated.

'I took lots of walks in Central Park, and there was one stage when I said to Greg, "Your career is progressing really well but things aren't going so well for me," and there was an offer to go back and take up my old job in Australia. That put us in a difficult position.'

Medcraft has worked for Société Générale, the parent company of S. G. Cowen, for nearly twenty years. It has always looked after him, and this time it looked after Binnie too: a position perfect for her became available in one of its subsidiaries. She started work in the United States in August 2001.

'They were prepared to process the visa for me,' Binnie remembers. 'That was about the time I was thinking, "Maybe I should go back to Australia." It's difficult to be put in the situation where you really have to make a choice between your personal life and your career. The job made me feel more independent. It gave me my own income and it did make me feel more a part of the community because I was working predominantly with Americans. I had a much closer link to the country I was living in. It wasn't a great career boost for me, but I was so pleased to be working.'

Four years later Binnie and Medcraft are the proud parents of baby Chloe, born early last year, and Binnie is on maternity leave. While she misses the company of her workmates, her days are kept busy in an entirely different way. It's a popular option among Australian couples who live in the United States. The inability of one partner to work does offer a chance to be a stay-at-home parent, but having a child in America also gives rise to a raft of fresh issues: do you want to raise your child in the United States? What is the American education system like? If you are living in New York City, would you prefer your child to attend a school where there is actually grass and a playground? Many New York schools have no yards; police sometimes block streets off on school days so children can play on the road.

From his own experience, Altria Group's Geoffrey Bible believes the Australian education system compares well with that in the United States. Bible attended Sydney's Waverley College but left at 14 without matriculating, later qualifying as a chartered accountant before embarking on a career that culminated in eight years at the helm of one of the world's biggest companies.

'In the nine years I was at school I reckon I was pretty well educated from a worldwide perspective,' Bible says. 'I was lucky. In my day you didn't need to have your matriculation to become a chartered accountant, and I really felt I could hold my own against the Harvard MBAs without any difficulty at all.'

When he was based in Switzerland, first with the United Nations' International Labour Organization and then with Philip Morris (the company's name was changed to Altria Group in 2001), his own children attended boarding school in England. Bible still believes England has 'the best education system in the world'.

'My granddaughter is going to state schools in England and it is absolutely outstanding. I'm not sure college here has the high quality that university has in Australia. I think you graduate from university in Australia in much better shape than you do here. But I think it more than catches up at postgraduate level.'

Binnie and Medcraft's daughter seems certain to receive an Australian education. 'I absolutely assume I'll go back [to Australia],' Binnie says. 'It has been great working in America, a fabulous experience. It's such a broadening experience for people. But I really love Australia and my family's there and my friends are there and I really want to continue my life. I'd definitely like Chloe to be brought up with an Australian accent. I was determined to go back before, but I think if anything Chloe has made me more determined.'

Robyn McKanna had a similar experience to Binnie on arriving in the United States in 1999 with her husband. A former journalist turned public relations professional, Guy McKanna had been offered a position with New Jersey–based NUS Consulting and the couple arrived as many Australians do: he held a work visa by virtue of his new job; Robyn did not. Being in the United States as what is called a 'non-resident alien' brings a host of problems.

'The biggest issue for me was not having a social security number,' Robyn says. 'As Guy was extremely busy in his new role, my job was to take care of everything else. Without a social security number, and with the status of "non-resident alien", I basically didn't have a valid identity when it came to any official business. Despite my intentions of helping out my spouse and taking care of all our administration, I was unable to set up a bank account, get the telephone, gas or electricity connected, lease a car or get a credit card, as all of these things required a social security number. After twelve months or so I finally managed to get a store credit card with [department store] Macy's. It felt like I had won the lottery as I clutched the gold and black store card in my hand. After that my name and details were broadcast to just about every financial institution in the USA and I became the recipient of a mountain of junk mail from organisations offering credit cards and finance. Normally I would take offence at having so much junk mail, but in this instance it didn't matter. Finally I had grown beyond the status of "alien" and had once again become a "person".'

For a more authentic experience of American life, the McKannas chose to live in suburban New Jersey rather than nearby New York City. Robyn describes the experience overall as 'fantastic'. Life in America seemed a long way from Sydney's northern suburbs, where they now live after returning to Australia in 2003. 'I met some fabulous Americans who have become friends for life. True friends who cross the borders of time and distance,' she says. 'I became a Brownie leader, which, much to my astonishment, carried a huge amount of status in the local community. But, more importantly, it was fun to participate in traditional American celebrations and traditions. I even learned the "Star Spangled Banner" and the Pledge of Allegiance. In essence, my experience was of seeing the true America, not America through the eyes of an expat confined to an expat community.'

That social and cultural immersion can make returning to Australia even more difficult. Robyn McKanna found returning to Sydney after more than four years in the United States was more difficult than leaving, although she had always believed, 'because I was born in Australia and am a fifth-generation Australian, that the move back home would be easy'.

'It wasn't,' she says. 'The experience in New York had changed me. Yes, I was Australian, but I was now also a global citizen with eyes wide open. I realised that we have a wonderful country in Australia too, but it is not the only "paradise" on this planet. There are many other places that have incredible things to offer.'

Australians working in the United States whose partners were, at least initially, unable to do the same are unstinting in their praise of their partners. Peter Lowy, the chief executive of Westfield America, moved to Los Angeles in 1990 with his wife, Janine, and two daughters. The couple has since had two more children — a son and a daughter — and the globetrotting Lowy acknowledges the difficulties moving creates for partners and children.

'In the end I really give all the credit to my wife. It is very difficult for your spouse when you move as we did. While I was able to go to work and be fully engaged, Janine had to take care of two small children and rebuild our lives. With all our family still in Australia, she was able to create a very different life from the one we were used to. When we arrived in March 1990 we knew virtually no one, and while it was difficult in the beginning, we did spend all our free time together as a family unit and over time we were able to integrate into the community, with most of the burden falling on Janine to recreate our social life and lifestyle.'

The Lowys would also have to become quickly acquainted with an aspect of American life people without children can largely avoid — the education system. As Greg Coote puts it: 'What is the difference between freshman, sophomore, junior and senior? It's a whole new thing.' For the record, a 'freshman' is a first-year student at high school, college or university; a 'sophomore' a second-year student; a 'junior' a third-year student; and a 'senior' a final-year student.

Fortunately for him, Coote had an inside advantage: his wife is American. James Gorman has now lived in the United States for 20 years; his wife is American, and his two children are dual citizens.

Gorman's oldest child has been to Australia four times, the youngest three, and they will travel there again this year.

'They're very proud of the fact — I call them half-Aussie. But it is a foreign country to them still.' After his long residence there, Gorman's knowledge of America is much more advanced. 'I've been a little league baseball coach. I'm on the boards of both my kids' schools. I've served in various not-for-profit charitable institutions over the years. I feel I understand the culture very well — everything from sports to politics. You can't help that, after 20 years. I probably understand more about what's going on in this country than I do about Australia. No question in my mind.'

There is almost no news from Australia in the US media, unless it is something sensational, like a crocodile attack, or it happens to involve a prominent American. Without wading through online news sources every day to keep on top of events, Australians can quickly become detached from their homeland, while their perspective can be skewed by domestic US events. It is almost impossible not to feel detached from Australia when living in another country, particularly in the world's most dominant and influential.

'If it weren't for the Internet, I'd be less in touch,' says the *New York Post*'s Col Allan. 'I see things about Australia now that I couldn't have seen when I was there. I hate being critical — I think there are so many good things down there — but I don't see a national imagination about the future. I think the political argument in Australia is always tactical — there isn't a strategic political discussion going on down there. It's all about who's in power, who's going to appoint who to what job, instead of really imagining the future for the country and its people. I see that very, very clearly from here. It's a failure of the political class. I think America has been blessed with great riches. But its greatest resource, of course, has been the people, most of whom are not American at all. America has really understood that it's human capital that builds the future, and I don't understand these sorts of forces in Australia that can't see that — that want to keep the country almost colonial, in a sense, stuck down there, very safe.'

While many Australians living and working in the United States choose to return when their children start school, others who have moved to America with school-age children see big advantages. The children of Allan and his wife, Sharon, have basically become New Yorkers.

'To listen to them now, you'd think they were born here,' Allan says. 'I think it was academically difficult because the curriculum is very different, particularly for the older boys, who are teenagers. But, you know, kids are very resilient and much swifter to change than adults. I think the great thing for them is just being able to walk the streets of New York City. I have one of my sons who's constantly being thrown out of Barnes & Noble up on Broadway because he goes in there with his own bookmark and he reads books. It's just not the sort of thing a 12-year-old kid would do in Sydney, for some reason.

'Whenever we go back to Sydney we're struck by how white the city is. Now this will come as a great shock to people there, but it is true that in a melting pot of the planet like New York you get used to diversity. You go somewhere like Sydney, particularly, and there's a stark difference as you walk down the street. I think it's very good for kids to be in an environment where there are different races and different cultures, because I think it breeds tolerance.'

7 THE LAST MEN STANDING

Geoffrey Bible was born in 1937 into a family of Irish origin; his grandfather on his mother's side was born in 1863 on the ship coming out to Australia, and he has traced his father's family as far back as 1849. They are, Bible says, 'original Aussies'.

'I was born in Canberra before the war, and during the war we moved to Sydney, so I went to Waverley College. Then I left school and qualified as a chartered accountant. I was quite young — 21 — and I was broke like everybody was. The war hadn't been over that long and inflation was nothing anyone knew about. You bought a house in 1946 for £4000 and you sold it in 1956 for £4000. Prices didn't change. So to get a shilling increase in your weekly pay, or three shillings, was quite something. It wasn't easy to save money or make a decent living. All my friends somehow or another — probably because they had more means in their family — were able to go overseas and see the world. In those days it was by ship, as aircraft were rare things and they took a long time to get to England. And England was the place most kids went.'

Bible wanted to go overseas; the question was how. While he was making ends meet working as an accountant, he figured he wouldn't 'make a buck for the next ten years because I was too young to be made a partner'.

'My primary motivator was to see the world,' he says. 'I loved my work: I worked as a professional chartered accountant and I felt I did a pretty good job. But when you're young you want to get up and go and I was flat broke. When all your mates are going off and seeing the world, you're a bit restless.'

He answered a newspaper advertisement for jobs with the United Nations Relief and Works Agency for Palestine Refugees (UNRWA), the relief and development agency established in the aftermath of the 1948 Arab-Israeli war. The organisation provided education, health-care, social services and emergency aid to millions of Palestinian refugees created by the conflict. Some four million Palestinians are still helped by it today. But perhaps most importantly for Bible, the job would pay his way out of Australia. He was talked into applying by his best mate, fellow accountant Bill Murray, but it was Murray who actually scored a job and landed in Beirut in 1959.

'He got the job, but when he got there they said, "Do you know anybody else?" and he said, "Yeah, my mate," so I sent my form in and they asked me to come over and I did. I spent five years in Beirut, Damascus, Amman and the Gaza Strip, and that was a big learning experience. After five years I decided to return to Australia, because I'd saved a bit of money. They [UNRWA] had paid my fare over, and that got me out of Australia. I arrived there with hardly anything in my pocket but I did okay. I decided to come back and lined up a job, but on the way I met my wife in London, fell in love and, to cut a long story short, married her a year later and got a job in Switzerland.'

As might be suspected, the full story is significantly more inter-esting than that. Bible had decided to return to Australia via London, flying to Colombo, the capital of Ceylon (in 1972 renamed Sri Lanka), before catching a ship to Australia. In London he went to a party and spent most of the evening chatting with a New Zealand mate in the kitchen, not wanting to socialise. However, his friend had invited several other people to dinner, among them a woman Bible instantly fell for. Her name was Sara and she was Scottish, a widow and single mother of a young child, her husband having been killed in a mountaineering accident a year earlier. The evening before Bible was due to leave England he took her out on a date, and he landed back in Beirut raving to his mate Bill Murray about the woman he had left behind. Murray had a practical solution: send her a telegram saying you'd like to see her again and, if she agrees, head back to London for two weeks and then fly to Australia. The boat could wait. Sara's reply was music to Bible's ears: 'Would love to see you again'.

'I got back to London like a bullet!' Bible says. He still returned to Australia, but he didn't last long. 'Oh, I went back because I'd got this job, but I was only there for three months because to try to conduct a romance over the telephone in those days was impossible. You had to go to the post office and they'd say, "Wait in booth three." An hour later they'd say, "England — ticket number 643, booth three," and you'd get a phone call. Forget it. And Sara wasn't all that keen to come to Australia, so I said, "It's no problem for me," and I went back to the UK after three months.'

Geoff and Sara Bible now live in Greenwich, Connecticut, a wealthy, leafy town an hour north of Manhattan. After 18 years in the same house they recently moved, and while it wasn't a big move geographically — just down the road, really — personally it was a valuable one: among the couple's possessions, Bible found Sara's reply to his telegram from Beirut. He plans to frame it as a fortieth wedding anniversary present.

On 1 September 2002 Bible retired after eight years at the helm of one of the world's biggest tobacco and food groups, Philip Morris Companies. His staff were sad to say goodbye to a man who managed the seemingly impossible feat of keeping them motivated and proud of their work in an industry that was almost constantly under assault. For Australia, too, it marked the end of an era: the retirement of a man who was part of a pioneering generation of Australians leading America's corporate icons.

Australians had led American companies before — Bible's best friend, Bill Murray, had preceded him as chairman of Philip Morris — but never in such numbers: among others, the Coca-Cola

Company was headed by Douglas Daft, the Ford Motor Company by Jacques Nasser and McDonald's Corporation by Charlie Bell. Nasser had gone a year earlier, sacked in favour of Ford family member William Clay Ford, Jr; Daft retired at the end of 2004; and Bell succumbed to cancer early last year at the age of just 44. Bible's retirement was confirmation those days were over. While he does not see himself as a trailblazer, there is little doubt that the eminence of these executives inspired the generation of Australian professionals who now populate the upper echelons of corporate America in ever greater numbers.

At Bible's farewell, his Philip Morris colleagues presented him with a World Series cricket bat signed by the Australian and West Indian teams, along with a signed Wallabies rugby jersey. Both gifts tell you a lot about a man who, despite living outside the country for the better part of forty years, remains fiercely Australian. Arriving at his office in Greenwich, visitors won't find Bible's name on the door. Instead, three companies are listed: Wagga Enterprises, Maitland Enterprises and Riverina Enterprises.

'Every other name I thought of had been taken!' Bible says. 'But I still have a great affection for Oz — I'll die an Australian. I'm a US citizen too, but I'll die an Australian first of all. It's what you grow up with. You never forget it.'

In his spacious office, the 68-year-old keeps statues of cricketer Don Bradman and boxer Les Darcy, noting proudly that his grandfather 'carried a Les Darcy bucket or sponge or towel or something' before relating the tragic story of arguably Australia's greatest boxer.

It says something about the eternal allure of Australia that so many expatriates cling so tightly to their origins. Bible still has an Australian accent, albeit one mellowed by years of living in Europe and America. And you could scarcely find a better example of the ambition and spirit of adventure that drives so many to leave Australia to forge careers overseas.

After returning to London and Sara, Bible began working for another United Nations group, the International Labour Organization

(ILO), in Geneva, Switzerland. His experience at the ILO compared poorly with UNRWA. With a mandate focusing on labour issues and social justice, the ILO was founded in 1919 as an agency of the League of Nations and then became part of the UN on its creation following World War II.

'I was there a year before a mate of mine I played squash with said they were looking for an accountant at Esso,' Bible says, referring to the energy group now owned by ExxonMobil Corporation. 'They were great. I worked very hard and they promoted me very quickly, and then they decided to blow up the whole office and spread the survivors to England, Nairobi, Athens and Casablanca. I'd had enough of deserts so I decided to go back to Australia again. Just before I left, I went to a cocktail party and met a Scotsman there and asked, "What do you do?" and he said, "I'm the executive assistant to the executive vice president at Philip Morris International." He asked, "What do you do?" and I said, "I'm an accountant but I just lost my job because they've blown up this company. They've offered me other jobs but not what I want to do so I'm going back to Australia." He said, "We've just opened up here. Maybe I'll give you a call." Anyway, I ended up taking a job at Philip Morris.'

Bible joined the tobacco company in 1968 as its financial head for Europe, the Middle East and Africa. He left in 1970 to join Australian broking house Ralph W. King Yuill in Geneva but returned six years later, brought back by his friend Murray, who had himself been lured to Philip Morris by Bible.

'In 1978 Philip Morris asked me to come here [the US], and I lived here for two or three years and then they sent me back to Australia to run the company down there, in Melbourne. I came back here in 1984 and moved up through the ranks.'

He makes it sound easy, yet when initially offered the US role he was in two minds. 'I didn't really want to come. We were very, very, very happy in Switzerland, and our children — two of our children — were at boarding school in England, which was just a hop, skip and a jump away. My wife had family there, so the kids could see them. It was a bit wrenching. So the plan was that I'd come here for just a few years and then go back to Europe. I had to dynamite my wife out of Switzerland; now I can't dynamite her out of here! So I came here and a year later she followed, then all three kids were going to boarding school as I wasn't sure what was going to happen with my life and whether I would go back to Europe. Well, what happened is I was here for three years and then went to Australia and then came back here again. So it never quite worked out that way.'

Bible was managing director of Philip Morris Australia for three years before returning to the United States in 1984. By 1994 he had taken the helm of the company — since renamed Altria Group — most recently ranked by *Forbes* magazine as the world's twenty-fifth largest, with a market value of more than US$134 billion. Under Bible, operating income almost doubled to US$17.3 billion, earnings per share grew at a compound rate of 12 per cent, and the company outperformed Standard & Poor's 500 Index by generating an annual return of 14.3 per cent. Not bad for someone who never envisaged coming to America.

Thinking back to his departure from Australia as a 21-year-old, Bible recalls, 'The world was a bit different then: it was a much smaller place. When I flew from Sydney to Beirut I was in the one aircraft, a Super Constellation, for 45 hours. And it was a bit more civilised: in Karachi, they took you off the plane, took you to a hotel, let you have a shower and a sleep for four or five hours and then brought you back to the plane. In Karachi for breakfast, they produced a box of Kellogg's Cornflakes and I thought, "Geez, looks like we export Cornflakes," because I thought Kellogg's was Australian. I saw Colgate and thought we must export Colgate toothpaste too. I had no idea these great trademarks were American trademarks.

'I think we almost felt at the time that America was beyond realistic hope. It was thought to be too expensive because the US dollar was very strong; none of us knew much about America. England we all knew about: all your mates had been there, and there was all this history with your parents and grandparents. The passport I got to go to Beirut was a British passport — it said, "British passport; citizen of Australia". So you were still very much oriented that way. And the attractive part of it was you could go and see Europe — get a Vespa and zip off and that was really quite romantic and interesting. So that part of the world held more attraction to us mainly because it was realistic.

'One of my mates went to America. His father was a big shot in Australia and got him a scholarship to Tennessee University to study cotton and we all thought, "What a knockout — fancy going to America!" It was almost beyond your dreams to go to America. It was too much. England was a little bit more ... you could probably afford it. In those days, communication was very limited and you didn't know much about the rest of the world.'

Young men of Bible's generation had little thought of fulfilling personal ambition or testing themselves against the world's best. He merely wanted to travel, fully expecting he would one day end up back in his homeland. However, as with many, knowing Australia was always an option should the overseas adventure sour lent him courage — or at least made him more prepared to go wherever opportunity took him.

'My theory was I could always make a buck. I figured I could always sweep the streets. I was never worried about being competitive — maybe that's a more recent phenomenon. In those days, I didn't look at it that way at all. I was young and I loved Australia very much. I always thought I could make a successful career in Australia no matter what. But once I was married, and because my wife is from the UK and her family situation is a bit more complicated than mine, I had no problem leaning in that direction. It was less complex to be in Europe. I'd already made the break and it wasn't a big deal. By then I'd been around the world a number of times, I'd gone home to Australia and back the other way, stopped off and seen other places, other cultures, and I thought the world was a fairly small place and no matter where you live you can meet people. Family takes over. If the world fell apart you could always go back to Australia. I knew that was always an option.'

While Bible acknowledges there's something in the suggestion that having Australia as a safety net makes expatriates braver, he also notes that once you have worked overseas for a given period, it becomes much harder to go back to Australia than to keep working internationally. Given his limited experience as a chartered accountant before leaving to join UNRWA, Bible admits 'there comes a point when you may no longer be relevant'.

'They'll say, "Well, what have you been doing for the past 15 years?" and you say you've been working in the desert in Siberia or something and they say, "Great, but that's not much help to us, fella." There's a point when you probably recognise that you've cut yourself out of the workforce in Australia. You could probably get a job as a cab driver or something, but to go back and start a professional career as a chartered accountant would have been difficult for me 20 years later.'

Men like Geoffrey Bible, Douglas Daft, Jacques Nasser, James Wolfensohn and Rupert Murdoch were trailblazers, carving careers in a country Australians had historically regarded as either too tough a nut to crack or not as appealing as the easy alternative, Britain. While Murdoch entered the United States by virtue of the relentless expansion of his News Corporation media empire, the rest worked their way up through industry ranks. Some, like Nasser, Daft, Bell and Dow Chemical's Andrew Liveris, stick with a single company all the way to the top.

It is difficult to underestimate the courage it takes to turn your back on your homeland for the uncertain and perilous road of working your way up through corporate America. It is a different professional and personal environment, and one that just two decades ago remained so different from Australia that it seemed, figuratively and literally, as far removed as it was possible to be. Yet the process of globalisation — which in part might be justly termed 'Americanisation' — helped level the playing field for executives from small English-speaking nations such as Australia, placing a premium on adaptability and international knowledge.

Bell is a prime example. He began working part-time at the McDonald's restaurant in the Sydney suburb of Kingston in 1975, aged 15. Just four years later he was the country's youngest store manager; by 27 he had risen to become a company vice president, and two years later he was director of McDonald's Australia. At that point his global development took off. He spent 1983 to 1985 working at McDonald's Europe development company in Frankfurt, Germany, dealing with joint-venture partners and licensees in countries including Sweden, Holland, Belgium and Norway. He was operations director and regional manager before becoming vice president of marketing in 1990, and he returned to Australia in 1993 as managing director of McDonald's Australia. He went back to run the company's European operations and was in 2003 elevated to the position of president and chief operating officer of McDonald's worldwide before succeeding CEO Jim Cantalupo after the latter's fatal heart attack in April 2004. Bell was in the top job only a month when he was diagnosed with cancer. He died in Australia eight months later, in January 2005.

You might think the opportunity to kick for the top of one of the world's iconic brands would have been incentive enough to leave Australia. Yet when Cantalupo began talking to Bell about running McDonald's Asia–Pacific operations in the mid 1990s, Bell spent three years trying to convince him to move the position to Sydney from the company's US headquarters in Oak Brook, Illinois, near Chicago.

'Jim, this is not a slam-dunk decision for me,' Bell told Cantalupo, according to *Business Review Weekly* magazine in 2003.

'Because if I make the decision to come to Oak Brook to take that role and give up managing director of Australia, I basically don't make a decision to relocate, I make a decision to emigrate.'

Cantalupo's response was instant. 'You wouldn't be brought here if I didn't think you had the capability to move much higher in the organisation,' he told Bell. 'If you want to be the Pope, you have to come to Rome.'

Bell's career was cut tragically short. But one of the truisms of corporate life is that it gets narrow at the top, and the level of accountability rises exponentially.

'Instinctively I knew that it was either this or the bullet,' Bible says of his rise to the top job at Philip Morris after years of being viewed as a potential corporation leader. 'I think a lot of people learn to live their lives like this — knowing that when you get to the top, you can wake up the next day without a job. It's a tightrope. And you walk this tightrope and one day they can say, "Sorry Geoff, here's your envelope," and that's it. So you're way up in the firing line. I hadn't thought where I would go if that had happened, but I guess I would have stayed here [in America].'

Ford's Jac Nasser discovered just how fickle a company's affections could be when, in 2001, his seemingly unstoppable rise to the top of the automobile group ended abruptly, partly owing to events beyond his control. Born in a mountain town north of Beirut in Lebanon in 1947, Nasser's family moved to Australia in the early 1950s and he studied business at the Royal Melbourne Institute of Technology before joining Ford as a financial analyst. In 33 years with the company, he lived and worked in many countries, including Australia, Thailand, Japan, South Africa, Venezuela, Brazil, Argentina, Mexico and throughout Europe, landing in Ford's top job in January 1999.

Nasser's appointment, just before his fifty-first birthday, was almost universally applauded and the company's share price peaked at US$65 shortly after he took over the helm. By the time he was ousted in October 2001, the share price had fallen by 75 per cent and the cheerleaders were gone. Nasser refused to bite back and insisted the barbs of his critics did not sting.

'In my wildest dreams I never thought about or fantasised about progressing through the Ford Motor Company as I did,' he told *AFR BOSS* magazine in 2003. 'I've got a basic belief that you're loyal to the environment you grow up in, whether it's a family or a culture or a country or a company, or the people that you grew up with. There were 380 000 people that made up Ford Motor Company ... I was very humble in my own way about who I was, and I represented them, and time goes on. You've got to look forward. I've always looked forward, I don't look back. A lot of people look to rewrite history. My own preference is to help create a better future.'

One of the primary factors in Nasser's downfall was what is now known simply as the Firestone scandal. It began when Ford's flagship four-wheel-drive vehicle, the Explorer, was involved in numerous rollover accidents. By the time the litigation dust settled, 200 deaths had been linked to accidents involving vehicles using Firestone's Wilderness AT tyres, which happened to be standard on the Explorer. In August 2000, Firestone — owned by Japan's Bridgestone Corp — announced the voluntary recall of about 6.5 million tyres, while Ford committed to replace millions more. It was a publicity nightmare for both companies, and Nasser's toughest test.

'I was put in a position where the integrity of the company was put into question and it was very difficult for the whole organisation,' Nasser said. 'Very few people in the management at the time had very much to do with what was going on. But I felt it was necessary at almost any cost to the company that we not only defend the integrity of the company, but also protect our customers and make sure that for the long-term the corporate reputation of the company and its people was protected. In my life at Ford it is probably the most challenging [event], but maybe also the best of times, because the true values and integrity of the people in the Ford Motor Company came out. I've dealt with a lot of companies. I've never seen anything in 33 years at the Ford Motor Company that I would feel ashamed of in terms of its values and business integrity. I see a period where the management team was focused and the whole company came through that with our reputation, our image, our integrity, and our relationship with our customers and stakeholders, probably stronger than before.'

It may have ultimately cost Nasser his job, but many expatriates express pride over the way he dealt with the Firestone problem. Even though the problem was due to the Firestone product and the design of a car determined ten years before Nasser assumed Ford's top job, he stepped up and took responsibility — as a chief executive officer should. And he spoke to customers and shareholders in a straightforward, distinctly Australian manner. As one top Australian executive noted, it also opened a few eyes to the role Australians were playing in the United States.

'One of the things that struck me with Jac Nasser was, when Ford had the problem with tyres and he went on TV, how many Australians said to me, "Where the hell did that guy come from?" ' says Ian Phillips, the former head of the Commonwealth Bank in the United States and now the institution's head of global bank partnerships. 'They couldn't believe an Australian was running an iconic American company like Ford.'

Geoffrey Bible sometimes finds it hard to believe he ended up running Philip Morris. It might be construed as false modesty, but a striking number of top Australian executives insist they were somewhat baffled by their rapid ascent through some of the world's biggest companies. Nearly all report simply doing their jobs as best they could, and being shocked that, when the management dust cleared, they were often the ones left standing. Having rejoined Philip Morris in Switzerland in 1978, Bible found himself occupying the giant company's top position just 17 years later. Was he surprised by his rapid rise?

'I didn't ever expect to be chairman and CEO, not in a million years,' he says.

'I thought there were better people ahead of me. And I thought, "I'm younger, they're older, and by the time they retire I'll be retiring too." But it's funny how life works. If you pick up any annual report that lists the executives and then have a look at the list the next year, you'd be surprised who's not on that list. People do just sort of fall off the ladder. And if you stay in ... I was the only guy left! At the time, that's probably what happened.'

Like many other successful expatriates, Bible adapted well to his environment. After living in Europe for so long, he didn't find the transition to America particularly difficult and the shared language made a big difference, as borne out by the number of top executives in the United States from English-speaking countries.

'The language was common, food was somewhat similar, entertainment was somewhat similar, religious activities were somewhat similar. Things worked much the same, so it wasn't a big shock.'

Indeed, Bible believes Australians are particularly suited to working for American companies in international positions, a view echoed by Australians who find the labyrinthine world of US office politics difficult to crack.

'My own sense is that Australians are better suited to American international companies than to the American domestic companies,' Bible says. 'So, for example, we have a huge international business and we had a lot of Australians working in that and I found them much more transplantable than many nationalities. Culturally more easygoing, they adapt very well to new conditions; they have a good disposition towards other nationalities; and they have a great ability to roll with the punches. I think they sort of realise that Australia is way out there and if you're going to do anything worthwhile in life, you're going to have to see the rest of the world. Going and seeing these kinds of places is a part of life. So I think Australians can be much more helpful to an American company that wishes to grow its international business.

'There's a plethora of very confident American executives here already but their ability to adapt overseas is not as good as Australians', I think. The culture here is not the same and more Australians see it as exciting and interesting to go abroad. Americans are more insular, there's no doubt about that. They find it's so attractive here: the kind of life, the success of colleges here — everybody here can go to college. But if you go and live in Malaysia or somewhere, you can't pull that off and that's a huge trade-off if you're an American. If you're Australian, you're a bit more, I'd say, internationally oriented. I think that's because we were a colony. We grew up out of England and most of us always wanted to go and see England and Europe and other places. Maybe it's an accident of history.'

Of course, working hard isn't a problem for Australians in America. While the popular image of Australians among Americans might be of the relaxed, laconic, knock-around guy sipping a beer and tending the barbie, the reality is that Australians tend to work until the work is done. It's not a matter of arriving at your desk early and leaving late just for the sake of being seen to be working hard. If the job is done, go home. But that also means staying as long as it takes when work demands it. Among all the professional culture issues he had to deal with, Bible recalled that his work ethic was simply 'not a problem'.

'Most of us work very hard and I'd been accustomed to that, as a personal culture. In fact, maybe a bit too hard. I remember one secretary who said, "He even made me work during my lunch hour!" She was really bent out of shape. But you need to be a bit careful about your language. I don't mean coarse language, but your expressions and phrases don't necessarily mean the same thing here. Certainly when I first came to America at Phillip Morris, my abruptness caused problems. It was an issue with people. It didn't particularly worry me because to me it was do it or don't do it, get it right or don't get it right. I wasn't very good at going into long descriptions. It was fairly clear-cut to me what had to be done, and if people weren't doing it properly I didn't have much patience with them. So to the extent that there was wastefulness or slothfulness or sloppiness, I would deal with that. I wouldn't say all Australians are like that; I was probably more blunt than most. It would be wrong to say all Australians are like that.'

Of all Australians' adaptations to living in the United States, one area typically remains off limits: relinquishing Australian citizenship. Until 2002, becoming an American citizen required giving up Australian citizenship, which resulted in a few Australians handing in their passports. The most famous example, of course, is that of Rupert Murdoch, who in 1985 swore allegiance to the United States to meet media ownership rules and allow the creation of his Fox television network. Bible is an American citizen but had never intended to become one, or to relinquish his Australian citizenship. His story is similar to Murdoch's, which is interesting given that the men are friends and have served together on the boards of their respective companies.

'I'm an Australian and I love being an Australian,' he says. 'But amongst our operating companies we had one called Capital Corporation. Capital corporations generally are created to develop deferred taxes — you pay the same taxes but you pay them later so you have the money in the bank for longer, so you earn interest. We bought powerhouses and leased them back to the government; we bought aircraft and leased them back to the airlines. You get accelerated depreciation, which enables you to have deferred taxes. The CFO [chief financial officer] at one time before I became CEO bought three Coast Guard ships and leased them back to the US Coast Guard. Turns out that there's a law somewhere that says the nationality of a Coast Guard ship is the nationality of its owner or the CEO of the company. So I've just been made CEO, I'm Australian and suddenly an Australian owns three Coast Guard ships, and that distressed the authorities. So they contacted us in a flap.

The counsel said, "Geoff, we have two options. You can become a citizen or we sell the ships and lose US$100 million." And I said, "Well, I'd better become a citizen." Now that sounds fake — like I was inveigled into it. In fact, I said I didn't want to give up my Australian citizenship, but in those days you had to. And I'm very pleased to be a US citizen.'

Bible and his wife now live happily in Connecticut with a second home in Bermuda. Although he imagined returning to Australia throughout the formative years of his professional career, Bible always seemed to end up being enticed to remain overseas. Even after three decades away, he considered retiring to Australia.

'I thought about it, yeah. I didn't plan this but as a result of our kids being educated in England, two of them have ended up living there permanently, so there's grandchildren and so on. I have lots of friends there and I'm on the board of a company there. Sara still has all her family in Scotland. Australia is such a moonshot away from all these places. And when you retire, you know you're in the pink zone so you want to look at your medical services and your doctors are here and they know your left leg better than you know it, so you're conscious of all this and I've got my guys here. You know your way around. My younger daughter lives here and she's become an American citizen. So we sort of got involved in the life here. But I go back to Oz every year — I go back for the rugby every year, pretty well. While I love Australia, you're closest to your family and where they're going and that takes over. I still have lots of mates in Australia and I go and see them — they're on sheep stations and whatever, and it's great fun. Now I can afford to do it and that helps, to know I can do that. But I don't have the close family ties.'

You get the sense Bible would do it all again exactly the same way. He rejects the suggestion that today it is easier to work overseas than in the past: it seems to be all about motivation.

'Well, I think if you wanted to work overseas you could always have got a job overseas. I'll give you an example: Just before I got the job to go to the Middle East [with UNRWA], I applied for a job at Pfizer, who were looking for internal auditors to go to Hong Kong. And they called me up and said to come in and they said, "Look, you're pretty young and you've got your degree, but why don't you spend a year with us here and then we'll send you overseas?" And I said, "That's not good enough — you might not. I like what I'm doing and if I want to go it's going to be over there, not here." And they said, "If you do go, why don't you drop by the Hong Kong office?" The bloke I had to see, it turned out he was on vacation, but later in life he lived 100 metres down the road from me and ran Pfizer International, an Aussie bloke. He's now retired. But you could, even then and that was in the fifties, you could always get a job overseas.

'If I was in Australia now and I was a 21-year-old chartered accountant, I would want to come here [to America]. I would probably choose to do a graduate course if I was 21 — although knowing what I know now, I wouldn't do it. I think it's a waste of time, frankly. But I would probably have thought it's good to do a graduate course and I would want to come here just because of the sheer volume of opportunities here in so many fields. They're so far ahead of the curve. Whether we like it or not, most things have their origins here and if you come here you'll learn so much more, so much more quickly. I always think that if you took that back to Australia five years hence, you'd be in great shape. Generally, though, once they've got you here and if you are any good and you've learnt it, they won't let you go! If they're smart, they'll say, "Why don't you go run our operations in Japan?" or something like that because we're good at that.'

Fundamentally, it seems the attributes of executives like Bible, Daft, Nasser, Bell and Liveris aren't that different from those they left behind. Australians, Bible believes, are 'very practical people'.

'They don't worry too much about ego and they can get on with the task in front of them, the task at hand. The world's not full of great stars, either. It's not that hard to make it here. Survival is very important, probably more so than brains. I look back on all the guys in my class at school and, you know, the smartest guys have turned out to be not very successful. If there were ten smart guys, one has been successful. The guys who have made it have been the plodders: they've been more stable, more sensible, more deliberate and practical.'

8 COMING HOME

In a real-estate market dominated by shoebox-sized apartments, this property was hard to miss: a five-storey former carriage house in Manhattan's Soho, dilapidated but sitting on a huge, 215-square-metre block. At night, fairy lights would appear in the windows and revellers at bars on adjacent Spring Street would wonder who lived there.

This was to be the New York home of Lachlan and Sarah Murdoch. The couple bought the property on a whim in 2003 after lunch at nearby eatery Bread, which reminds many Australians of a laid-back Sydney restaurant. Although Lachlan paid US$5.25 million for the building — the Commonwealth Bank provided a US$4.935 million mortgage — it required major structural work costing millions of dollars. The Murdochs rented in nearby Tribeca while architectural plans were finalised and the rumours flew: there was talk of a dog track to exercise the couple's pets (not true) and a lap pool in the basement (true). After two years, work was finally set to begin.

As fate would have it, the property did not become the permanent home of Lachlan and Sarah Murdoch. Instead, the couple moved back to Australia after Lachlan's shock decision in July 2005 to relinquish his executive roles within News Corporation, the media giant built by his father, Rupert. Lachlan, 33, forfeited his position — at least temporarily — as heir apparent to the US$50 billion empire, putting the succession pressure squarely on his younger brother, British Sky Broadcasting chief executive James Murdoch, 32.

'I will remain on the board and I am excited about my continued involvement with the company in a different role,' Lachlan said in a statement released by News Corporation at the time. He formally stepped down a month later but remained tied to the company by a two-year non-compete agreement. 'I look forward to returning home to Australia with my wife, Sarah, and son, Kalan, in the very near future. I would like especially to thank my father for all he has taught me in business and in life. It is now time for me to apply those lessons to the next phase of my career.'

Having watched one daughter, London-based Elisabeth, 36, strike out on her own by leaving News Corp to form the television production company Shine, Murdoch did not hide his disappointment. Since joining the family company in Brisbane in 1994, Lachlan had been viewed as his father's likely successor.

'I am particularly saddened by my son's decision and thank him for his terrific contribution to the company, and also his agreement to stay on the board and advise us in a number of areas,' Murdoch said. 'I have respected the professionalism and integrity that he has exhibited throughout his career at News Corporation.'

Just how long Lachlan pondered the decision is unclear. Just seven weeks earlier Sarah had given every indication the couple would be in New York City indefinitely, as much as they might wish circumstances were different. Lachlan's decision to return to Australia with his family was a shock, mainly because few people could imagine turning their back on running one of the world's most powerful media companies. Fending off the advances of John Malone, who has already snapped up 18 per cent of News Corp, would require a total commitment to the company — and a commitment to remaining in New York, where it is headquartered. The Murdoch children had spoken of seeing their father only intermittently as he built his empire; it appears that was a sacrifice Lachlan was not prepared to make.

The decision may not have been a total surprise to many within News Corp. The company's top executives were well aware of

Lachlan's strong affinity for Australia; indeed, many were puzzled by it given that he was born in London, raised and educated in the United States, and speaks with an American accent.

Lachlan moved to Brisbane in 1994 after graduating from Princeton University, New Jersey. He became general manager of Queensland Newspapers under the tutelage of John Cowley, the younger brother of former long-time News Limited boss Ken Cowley. By the time Lachlan arrived in New York in 2000, he had lived in Sydney, married and seemed to be on the carefully planned path that would take him to the top of News Corp. Yet there were persistent concerns in the financial community about the prospect of his taking the helm given his age and experience and the tough reputation of his father's number two executive, Peter Chernin. It must have seemed a no-win situation: thriving was the bare minimum for market acceptance; failing would draw brickbats and charges of nepotism. Rupert Murdoch has also shown few signs of relinquishing his grip on News Corp to allow an orderly transition.

Despite the pressure, there's no denying the News Corp unit most directly under Lachlan's control, the *New York Post* newspaper, has thrived. Since Lachlan became publisher and appointed former *Daily Telegraph* editor-in-chief Col Allan in early 2001, the newspaper has boomed — the once mammoth circulation gap with its major rival, the *New York Daily News*, has all but disappeared. While some of the sales growth can be attributed to halving the cover price to US25c — the *Post* is rumoured to still lose about US$40 million annually — much of its improved performance is due to genuine readership gains.

'His achievements include driving all of his reporting divisions to record profits and the *New York Post* to its highest-ever circulation,' Rupert Murdoch said last July. 'I am grateful that I will continue to have the benefit of Lachlan's counsel and wisdom in his continued role on the company's board.'

Even with that success and his ever-widening responsibilities as News Corp's deputy chief operating officer, fellow executives said

Lachlan would often talk about the possibility of returning to Sydney and run the global company from there. What seemed to many to be half-joking conversation was apparently anything but.

'I never thought I'd meet anyone more Australian than me or in love with Australia more than me,' Sarah Murdoch said of Lachlan in an interview with *WHO* magazine last June. 'He loves Australia and we just realise what an amazing country it is, especially when you live away for a long time.'

Australians living and working in the US grapple mightily with the decision whether to stay or return. It is a tough call for single people and even more difficult for those with families. Lachlan and Sarah's first child, son Kalan — Celtic for 'warrior', the name is taken from a character Lachlan used in short stories he wrote as a child — was born in New York in November 2004.

'I guess it started with marriage, those feelings of wanting to create a home and have a sense of permanence. Both of us travel so much and I felt like I never really had a home,' Sarah Murdoch told *WHO*. 'So I guess ... I mean, both of us now, all we think about is how we're going to get back to Australia one day. We have this dream of being able to live in Australia. When I tell [Lachlan] what it was like to grow up there — being on the beach, all the different sports, the outdoor lifestyle — we think about Kalan and what it would be like for him to grow up in New York. We're lucky we get to go home a lot and there's so many opportunities for us here, but when you have children everything else just pales and you want the best for your kids.'

A few months later the Murdochs bought a house overlooking Sydney's Bronte Beach for more than $7 million, jettisoning their $20 million Point Piper mansion because it was not as suitable for children. The building in Soho, New York, seems destined to remain unoccupied, at least for the time being. Just a week after dropping his career bombshell Lachlan happily walked off a plane from Tahiti. Tanned, relaxed and wearing a vintage Queensland State of Origin jersey and a pair of shorts, he seemed already to have switched back into the Australian lifestyle.

'It's cold,' he told *The Sun-Herald*, grinning. 'There's nothing that I really want to go into, but it's good to be off the plane. I'm gonna have some breakfast and then have a kip.'

For those who have spent their lives in a single city, it can be hard to appreciate the difficulties experienced by people whose work means they have to move around within Australia — the distance from family and friends, the unfamiliarity of new places, the time it takes to establish the small elements that collectively make life easier, such as the closest petrol station, supermarket, video store. Moving countries takes those difficulties to an entirely different level — the culture may be alien; you probably have fewer friends to lean on, no family and an overwhelming sense of unfamiliarity. In that respect, it might seem that moving back to Australia would be a breeze. Usually it isn't, although it may depend on how long you have been away.

'One of my cousins who came to the US in 1958 told me when I first arrived that four years is the tipping point,' says Morgan Stanley's James Gorman. Gorman has lived in the United States since 1985. 'If you've been away from your family and friends for four years, you've established new roots. It's harder to go back than to stay at that point. After four years it's easier to stay than it is to go back. I think he was about right.'

The degree of success expatriates experience on returning to Australia relates directly to which of the two types they are, according to the theory of DirecTV's David Hill. There are Australians, Hill argues, who spend all their time overseas awaiting the day of their return, dwelling on their nationality at the cost of the country they are in. The second type of expatriate is eager to blend in and learn about the country they have adopted — even if it is only temporary. The McKanna family falls into that second category.

In 1999 Guy McKanna was working for Sydney's Capital Public Relations. A former journalist with *The Australian Financial Review*, McKanna had spent time working with US company NUS Consulting, which specialises in helping companies reduce utility and telecommunications costs. Impressed with his work for them, NUS asked McKanna to move to America and become the company's director of marketing at its New Jersey headquarters. McKanna had always lived and worked in Sydney, apart from stints in Hong Kong as a public relations consultant. Hong Kong held some appeal as a place to live, London did not, but New York was the preferred choice.

'We got one trip over together to see if we were going to go or not,' McKanna says. 'Then we came back to Sydney and we all went over together. We stayed in a hotel for too many weeks — a month in a one-room hotel in Spring Valley — then we found the house in New Jersey.' The McKannas lived in the New Jersey suburb of Ho-Ho-Kus, a Native American term meaning 'red cedar', near a New Jersey Transit railway station to New York City. 'We decided to go not only because the company was based in the burbs but because we wouldn't be doing the expat thing in the city,' McKanna says. 'We wanted to be immersed in the culture.'

After just more than a year at NUS, McKanna was offered a job with Merrill Lynch in its office at the World Financial Center in downtown Manhattan, right next to the World Trade Center. He joined the investment bank in 2000 as a vice president of corporate affairs, responsible primarily for liaising with the hundreds of foreign journalists based in New York. McKanna regarded the job as more prestigious at a superficial level, although 'it was sort of a backward step to be international corporate affairs person out of New York rather than director of marketing'.

When he took the NUS job, he was unsure how long they would stay. 'I thought we'd do a couple of years but we were always very open-ended.' Switching to Merrill Lynch altered that time frame — he was now part of a bigger company with significantly greater prospects for advancement. 'But then you had the collapse of the IT bubble, and 9/11, which we were 100 metres away from. We got past the year after 9/11 but there was definitely an anti-foreign thing going on in New York City at that time — definitely at Merrills. I didn't really want to stay because there just wasn't any work. So I put my hand up for some money and we came home. We were there for four and a half years in the end.'

McKanna did not particularly want to return to Australia but soon resigned himself to that fate. 'We'd made the mental switch because there just wasn't any work in the US. I think we would have stayed there if a good job had come up.' The decision appeared to be made easier by a job offer from MLC, the wealth management division of National Australia Bank, before his time at Merrill Lynch had ended. The only problem was that a verbal telephone proposition is quite different from a formal, written offer. It was a almost year after returning to Australia in August 2003 before McKanna finally began at MLC, although in the interim he had done some work for Deutsche Asset Management's Asia–Pacific corporate affairs unit.

'It was easier for me because I found a job fairly quickly,' McKanna says of their transition. 'Just coordinating everything was difficult. We'd done our homework and knew it would be tough going back, but it was much tougher than we'd thought.'

His wife, Robyn, did not work while the family was in the United States and found the time away reignited her 'passion to keep growing and learning'. She is not working in Sydney now and the couple's children have settled back into school. 'When you return you are more of a global citizen,' she says. 'You realise there are other places in the world that are wonderful and great to live in. Australia does not have a monopoly in this respect and Australians have to realise this.'

The McKannas moved back into their old house in Vaucluse, but they quickly realised it had become too small. They now live in Castlecraig, in Sydney's northern suburbs. There were other problems settling back into life in Australia.

'You come back and some of your friends have moved on, or I guess you've grown a lot and they haven't,' Guy says. 'They're doing the same things and you've got more experience. I think I was smart in that I kept a lot of contacts via email while I was away. There are some friends here who are just the same as ever, and that's when you really realise who are good friends and who are just around.'

Professionally, McKanna feels he has much more experience to draw on following his years in America, although he has found that a few people think he is a 'smart-arse' when he starts talking about the work he did at Merrill Lynch. However, he has noted that work in Sydney is mostly comparable to that in America; in many respects, he believes he is doing superior work in his current role as the Sydney corporate affairs manager for National Australia Bank, including working with the company's business and private banking unit, which McKanna says is an operation of comparable scale to the seventh largest company in Australia.

'You've got to find the right job. That's the key,' he says. 'I can bring in my skills to challenge them to do things better. I think we're doing some things that are much better than what we were doing at Merrill Lynch. But you've really got to find that job when you come back. One of the things I'm enjoying about my work is that one day it might get me a position back in the United States. We're doing some great private banking stuff that is really world class.'

How does the pace of business compare? 'It depends who you work for. Some places the pace is definitely slower, some it is faster,' McKanna says. 'You reach a point in the US in a bigger company where you can only do so much and go so far if you're not local. If you're local, you probably play the politics better. There came a point where I just didn't get some of the politics. What I've done since coming back is find a role in which I can do things I wouldn't do in the US — which in a couple of years US firms are going to look at and think, "Geez, we need that."

'That's why I think you can come back to some Australian companies and sure, they're big, but they're flatter in management. The ones that tend to take the foreigners [in America] do tend to want to get things done. They want to have a competitive advantage and one of the best ways for some of the firms to do that is to get some Australians in.'

On a personal level, McKanna is relishing the ability to spend time with his family and the fact they live so close to the centre of Sydney yet are surrounded by native bushland. Although he enjoyed a relatively rural lifestyle in New Jersey, his commute to work would take about an hour. He lists some advantages of being back in Australia.

'The first is quality of life: spending time with the family. In New York you have weekends but you're working all the time, so you don't really. Second, the weather. We're in the middle of winter here and I just went canoeing in Middle Harbour. But that also means the skiing is shit, and you don't really get the seasons. Food is definitely better. Food really is much better here.'

Conversely, McKanna misses the people — 'Some of our American friends are the best people you'd ever meet' — and the sense of opportunity. It was also cheaper to live in the United States, where personal income tax rates are generally lower and many everyday necessities are cheaper. 'We found we had much more money in our pockets after tax there. The quality of education in the burbs was good and petrol was cheap. In New York itself, every corner is different and, not having grown up there, it was always interesting just to go there.'

After 21 years in the United States, David Evans is about to take the same step as McKanna. The 65-year-old is leaving his job as president and chief executive officer of Crown Media Holdings for a career familiar to many former top executives — as a professional director. Last year he was named to the board of newspaper publisher John Fairfax Holdings, prompting much speculation about the company's plans given that Evans' career has been spent entirely in the television business. He remains torn about the decision to leave America.

After a year in Toronto when he began his career, Evans spent seven years, up to the early 1980s, running Channel Nine in Melbourne for Kerry Packer. As with fellow media executive David Hill, working in the Australian television industry proved a more than adequate foundation for competing in the world's biggest entertainment market. Evans came to the United States in 1983 and stayed for nine years, at one point running Christopher Skase's Qintex Entertainment. In 1992 he moved to London to join Rupert Murdoch's British Sky Broadcasting, which had been created two years earlier by the merger of Murdoch's Sky Television and British Satellite Broadcasting. Working within the Murdoch empire allowed Evans to return to the United States two years later as president and chief operating officer of News Corporation's Fox Television, overseeing Fox Broadcasting Company, Fox Television Stations and Fox's FX cable channel. In July 1996 he became executive vice president of News Corporation in the United States and established the satellite pay television group Sky Entertainment Services Latin America.

Evans had another ambition: he wanted to create a pay television channel. After joining Tele-Communications International as president and chief executive officer in 1997, he approached Hallmark Cards about creating a subscription television service offering broad family entertainment that would appeal to the greeting card company's customers. Evans was made president and chief executive of Hallmark Entertainment Networks in 1999, and the Hallmark Channel is now viewed around the globe.

'I've been here for 21 years. When I came over I really didn't intend to stay that long,' Evans says. 'I always thought that I would end up moving back to Australia, mainly for family reasons. I have three children living in Australia and I have two sisters and nephews and nieces; my mum's still alive; and I've got a lot of friends. You think, "At some point I want to be back there and enjoy their lives with them.' I always had it in the back of my mind that I wanted to be back with my family at some point.'

One complication is that Evans has an American wife. That makes his decision to move back home quite unusual: typically, the person who has made the break from his or her homeland is the one who stays, rather than a spouse undergoing the same upheaval.

'My wife is very family-oriented and she has a brother here,' Evans says. 'She actually drove this move [back to Australia], not me. I would have been still saying, "Yes, we're going to go back one day," but she finally said a couple of years ago, "If we're going to make this move, for our daughter's sake, we need to make it now."'

Evans' wife and teenage daughter are already back in Sydney. He is living in Los Angeles and regularly commuting back and forth as he completes the work he has begun at Crown Media, which will take up to a year before he finishes 'doing what I'm doing now to my satisfaction'.

'I don't want to just walk out the door,' he says. 'Creating the channel was an idea that I had, that I took to Hallmark. When that's done, yes, I'll be moving to a situation where I could accept some directorships as well as some other things. Certainly I hope to be able to contribute to Fairfax's future. It's widely known that they'd like to expand their horizons.

'My family is very close. We all have a very close relationship and from that point of view I'm really enjoying my time back there [in Australia]. I've been commuting since last September [2004]. The travelling is a bit tough. As for moving back 100 per cent, I'm looking forward to it personally; unquestionably I am. From a business point of view, my honest answer would be I still have trepidations.' That said, Evans can see Australia's appeal. After two decades of testing himself in the home of the world's television industry, he has nothing left to prove. 'When you do go down to Australia, you look at the way people live and it's one hell of a lifestyle.'

The lure of the Australian lifestyle is strong, even for the most international of executives. Another who has returned after three decades of overseas postings is Ian Phillips, the head of global bank partnerships for the Commonwealth Bank of Australia. It seems an entirely appropriate position for a man who spent 30 years moving between London, New York and Sydney.

Born in New Zealand, Phillips began at the Bank of New Zealand and got his first taste of working overseas when he went to the bank's London office in 1975. He returned to New Zealand in 1977 but was on the move again just two years later, settling in New York City when the Bank of New Zealand opened an office there.

'I stayed there for three years,' he says. 'I went back to London for about a year and then I came back to New York for another couple of years.' He returned to Sydney in 1983 after then Treasurer Paul Keating floated the Australian dollar, ending its peg with the United States dollar and heralding a new era of foreign exchange trading. Since then the Australian dollar has become one of the world's most traded currencies, and Phillips has developed right alongside it, having made a conscious decision to develop an expertise in what was, 30 years ago, a somewhat obscure field.

'What I saw was the opportunities around foreign exchange. It would be a changing market and something that Australia and New Zealand would both have to do. So I tried to build an expertise in that area. I went to Sydney when they freed up the currency ... and stayed here until 1986, when I got hired by the State Bank of Victoria to go to London. They wanted to change their branch there from a retail to a wholesale branch, and I stayed there for about three and a half years and went back to New York when the Commonwealth Bank took over the State Bank. I came back to Australia in 1991 and then went back again in 1996.' He spent the next seven years as the Commonwealth Bank's executive vice president and general manager for the Americas, running its US operation.

What Phillips had done was identify a career path early and let his expertise do the rest: although he was headhunted for the State

Bank of Victoria position, all his other jobs resulted from internal appointments. He lobbied for overseas positions to develop his career and the banks' foreign exchange operations. There were 'great opportunities to make money but it tended to be that the banks in those early days were pretty risk averse'. Those bets paid off.

'Life is a little about luck and being in the right place at the right time. Going from New Zealand — although I had had a couple of years in London — to New York was a huge difference. The population of New Zealand at that time was about three and a half million and New York was 11 million or whatever. The number of people on Fifth Avenue was staggering. I remember walking with an old boss of mine in the early 1980s and I said, "There are more people walking here on a Monday morning than there are in Gore on a Friday night."' Gore, the small town in New Zealand's South Island where Phillips is from, has a population of about 12 000 people. New York City's subway system, by comparison, carries more than 4.5 million people daily.

Arriving in such a large city and working for such a small financial institution (by Wall Street standards) presented problems: how do you make contacts or get noticed? 'In the late seventies I got a letter from a public relations company and they said, "Dear Ian, blah blah … for the sum of $5000 we will be able to introduce you to specific people in the financial markets world in New York and you'll get invited to crucial parties and functions." I ripped it up, thinking, "What a rip-off!" But that may have been a huge mistake, because who you know is everything.'

Fortunately he didn't need a public relations firm to do his networking for him. Gregarious by nature, Phillips ended his time in New York in 2003 as one of the city's most well-connected expatriate professionals, heavily involved in the American Australian Association (AAA). Even 30 years ago the networking had begun — at an unlikely bar on Manhattan's Second Avenue, The Green Derby. Phillips and his colleagues used to have after-work beers there — sadly the bar no longer exists — and he soon met other financial industry professionals, such as John Meriwether, who was then at Salomon Brothers.

Meriwether went on to become one of Wall Street's most famous arbitrageurs, immortalised as an über–bond trader in writer Michael Lewis's 1989 book *Liar's Poker*. At the forefront of endeavours to bridge classical mathematics with the art of trading, Meriwether joined with economists Robert Merton and Myron Scholes, who in 1997 won the Nobel Prize for their work on pricing options, and created the hedge fund Long-Term Capital Management in 1994. The fund's initial returns were stunning: one American dollar invested in 1994 in LTCM was worth four dollars by early 1998. However, the arbitrage business is highly leveraged, and LTCM was exposed when in late 1998 the Russian government defaulted on its sovereign debt, prompting panicked investors to flee to the safety of US Treasury notes. The demand for the notes depressed their price, and LTCM went into a tailspin that resulted in a US$3.65 billion bail-out led by the Federal Reserve Bank of New York to prevent a wider collapse in financial markets. LTCM's total losses were eventually found to be about US$4.6 billion.

Phillips is unshakeable in his belief in the value of overseas experience, particularly in the United States. As chairman of the AAA's Australian advisory board, he is continuing to try to bridge the gap between the three countries.

'That's something I think is very important: to have a very strong relationship between the United States, Australia and New Zealand,' he says. 'If it's going to happen somewhere in the world, it's highly likely to happen somewhere in the US first, and there are advantages to understanding that early.'

Married in 1980 to an American, Phillips has three children: son Harrison, born in Sydney in 1985, and twin girls Nicole and Zara, born in London in 1988. The decision to return to Australia permanently was made for the sake of the girls, to allow them to complete high school in Sydney. (Harrison had boarded at Sydney's St Joseph's College.)

'We were pretty conscious we had to make that decision. If you leave your children to go through high school [in America] it tends to be very difficult to get them to come out and live in Australia afterwards. They become very Americanised, particularly in the high-school years.'

Phillips and his family moved back to Sydney in 2003. Having moved several times during his career, he knew of the problems traditionally associated with returning from an international position to the home office. 'It's difficult to go back. I was conscious of that before I ever left. The way I've always looked at it is when you leave, going off to do something else, that position is filled, so to come back a new position has to be created. Generally, banks have a pretty poor record of managing people who come back from overseas. They tend not to strategically map out careers like that. You have to think about it yourself.'

The solution is one many expatriates adopt: you create your own position. Phillips aimed to carve out a role that took advantage of his background as well as solving a problem for his employer.

'The Commonwealth Bank is a big regional bank here, whereas it was pretty small in the United States. So really you have to be in Australia,' he says. 'What I do is run our global banking relationship group, which is responsible for all the relationships we have around the world with other banks. So I travel a lot — I'm in New York three or four times a year. We thought it was a great opportunity to do more bank-to-bank deals in a more focused way. I proposed it [and] we agreed this was a very necessary role.'

Although Phillips had relocated to Sydney before, there has still been a settling-in period. During the seven years he was away he had made an effort to maintain friendships, but there is an 'adjustment in moving anywhere and you have to be conscious of that'.

'I think it always requires an adjustment to go from town to town, city to city, country to country. You don't always recognise how big that adjustment is. You have to carve out your position in life, whatever that may be: you've changed, you've had different experiences; and the people you've left behind have changed too. You can't help but make comparisons, but the glory of Sydney is it is an international city. It's a huge city. I lived twice in Manhattan and twice in Scarsdale [north of Manhattan], and if you're living out there, you're in the burbs.'

Moving to Sydney from Scarsdale was actually comparable to moving from the suburbs to the inner city. Phillips used to live opposite the general manager of the New York Yankees baseball team, Brian Cashman, in what was very much a leafy suburban neighbourhood, away from the stresses of Manhattan.

Having lived in London and tried to help many Australians living and working in America, Phillips believes the United States remains a more difficult destination to build a career.

'Definitely there's a bigger group of people, particularly professionals, looking to go somewhere like New York and the financial markets. They see that as a big part of their career progression. I think a lot of people still look to Europe — it's a tradition and there seems to be a better system in place when people get there. I don't know what it is in the United States, but it seems to be more complex for people there.'

Phillips has found that Australians and New Zealanders work overseas 'always with the intention — just about to a person, a conscious decision — that they will come home eventually'. The thought of settling permanently in the United States never really crossed his mind. In part this was a consequence of his loyalty to Australia and New Zealand, but it also relates to the fact that he had always worked for Australian companies. In that sense, the promotional path was in Australia, not the United States.

'The United States was not a place I wanted necessarily to retire in. I suppose the ideal would be to have a place in the United States and a house somewhere in this part of the world, and to be able to commute between the two.'

When his family arrived in Los Angeles at the start of his last American stint, they went shopping. The twin girls, used to having a handful of clothing options to choose from at stores in Australia, were stunned to discover American shops offering literally hundreds of choices. 'They were speechless; stopped in their tracks,' he recalls. It was an experience that Phillips believes encapsulates the difference between the two countries. 'My daughters finish high school at the end of next year and there's a strong likelihood of one of them, perhaps both, going to college in the US. There's a great opportunity for them to at least consider broader options.' America is not necessarily better than Australia, he feels; it just offers more choices.

9 CLOSING THE CIRCLE: THE LURE OF HOME

Greg Medcraft joined French banking giant Société Générale in Melbourne in 1987 and within a year found himself working at the company's headquarters in Paris. Securitisation was in its infancy then but is now a commonplace idea: it essentially involves bundling asset-backed loans, such as home mortgages, and selling them to a trustee, who receives interest generated by the assets' cash flow. The trustee then sells an interest in that cash flow to investors. Medcraft initially planned to be in Paris for a year; he ended up staying for three and playing an instrumental role in the establishment of Société Générale's European securitisation operation. In 1989 he was asked to head the company's global securitisation business. He declined.

'I chose to go back to Australia,' Medcraft says. 'My son is dyslexic and basically it was very hard for him to get what he needed in Paris, so we decided to return home and the bank created securitisation in Australia for me. So I went home to run a mixture of securitisation, project finance and M&A [mergers and acquisitions].'

A second consideration was Medcraft's eldest daughter, who was just two months old when he went to Paris. Determined to raise her in Australia, he told the bank he wouldn't consider moving overseas until she was at least 12 years old. Société Générale understood and respected Medcraft's wishes.

'That's why I'm still with them. They're a pretty good employer in that they totally understood the family situation,' he says. 'I left them in the lurch a bit. It was very rare for a non-Frenchman to be offered a position running a whole business, and back in 1989 it was almost unheard of. I had to decide to choose family and walk away from running the business globally.'

For the next nine years Medcraft was regularly asked whether he was prepared to move back to Paris. He still resisted, not just for his family's sake but also because the company was doing innovative work in Australia, while the European securitisation industry was largely treading water.

'It was always expected that I couldn't aspire to be the global head while based in Sydney. But we were doing interesting deals in Australia and Asia. We were doing quite innovative transactions in those days. When I left Europe my market was a fledgling one, and in that period I wasn't too worried because the European market really didn't go anywhere. At one stage the Australian business in securitisation was bigger than the European business, because we grew quite rapidly. One thing I did miss was seeing what was happening in the United States. But I did other things: I stood for council and was mayor of Woollahra and other stuff. I got involved in other things that gave me satisfaction, but it also meant I stayed in Australia, which was a good thing from a family perspective.'

In 1999 Société Générale knew Medcraft's daughter was turning 12. The call came and he finally acquiesced: two days after her birthday he left Australia for New York City to become the head of US securitisation for S. G. Cowen, the firm's investment banking unit. Tired of people asking why he was still in Australia when securitisation was huge globally, particularly in the United States, Medcraft was ready for a new challenge. 'I always said that having lived in Paris, I didn't really want to move back to Europe. If I had to move overseas, I'd rather move to the US. When the opportunity came up for the US job, I said, "Fine."'

The move was not without problems. Medcraft initially struggled to be accepted by his American counterparts but kept chipping away. His breadth of experience throughout Europe, Australia and Asia commanded respect and, in perhaps a final vindication,

Medcraft is now serving a three-year term as chairman of the American Securitization Forum, an industry body he helped found after arriving in the United States to discover there was no such organisation.

'Getting accepted by Americans was a bit of a challenge. There was a bit of conflict in the early days,' Medcraft says. 'I replaced an American and I think globally the business was trying to develop a more aligned strategy. One of the reasons they brought me in was because I had broken through in developing the market in Europe, then I'd gone back to Australia and done it in Australia, Japan, Hong Kong. This market had already been quite commoditised, so it was quite interesting because there was an opportunity to see where we could bring innovation.

'Increasingly, Australians access the global capital markets. So if you want to be based in Australia and you want to access this market you want to be working with somebody who has worked in these markets. The more challenges you expose people to, the more different ideas they'll have. If you've worked in Europe or America, you'll have seen things from a different angle. You'll have seen different ways of doing things. That's what working overseas is all about. You can make things happen that you couldn't have if you had only lived in and experienced Australia. Working overseas is just a great source of creativity, frankly. From that perspective, it's invaluable.'

In 2000 Medcraft took over as S. G. Cowen's global head of securitisation, a position he still holds. Having helped establish his firm's presence in Europe and throughout Asia, broadened its American market and represented the industry, it would seem there are few new challenges for him to aspire to. Medcraft's boss in the US recently retired — at the age of 48 — to go car racing, and he admits that is an option should he tire of the intellectual and professional challenge.

'In investment banking, you can just choose to retire,' Medcraft says. 'I guess you get to a point where if you really want to just retire or choose to do something different, there's an element of freedom in that. But I know a lot of people who keep working because they would be bored if they didn't and they like the dynamic. The interesting thing when you get to this sort of position is it's really exciting — you can actually think of strategies and put them into action. That's the benefit of being in management. There's always something to do.'

Yet Medcraft's next move is likely to be to return to Australia. For someone in his position at the relatively young age of 49, that probably means a senior role at an Australian bank, although he thinks you have to 'accept that if you want to go home it's probably to a different focus'. Another option is to take the helm of Société Générale in Australia, a position that comes up every few years under the bank's rotational management system. 'I'd be quite satisfied to do something like that,' he says.

'I'm not homesick because I have the business in Australia, so I go home twice a year,' Medcraft says, referring to his responsibility for the bank's Australian securitisation business. 'And I talk to Australia every night, so I honestly don't feel homesick. I felt much more homesick when I was in Paris. New York's a pretty easy place to live — the weather's not too bad and it's an amazing place to do business. The capacity to make money is manyfold greater than Australia because the market is so large, so it's an earning capacity issue as well.'

Medcraft and his wife, Kay Binnie, are also the proud parents of another daughter, Chloe, who was born last year. The couple have three houses in the inner-city Sydney suburb of Paddington and would like Chloe to grow up in Australia, which makes an eventual return more likely. 'I'm now in the mode where if the job in Australia, for example, came up, probably on the next rotation I'd put my hand up to go home,' he says of running Société Générale in Australia. 'The hardest thing when you do want to go home is finding the path to doing so. The more senior you are, the harder it is. It gets narrow at the top.'

His other option should not come as a surprise given his background, yet a surprising number of Australian expatriate executives mention it: politics. Medcraft has had two stints as mayor — of Box Hill in Victoria in 1985 and 1986 and Woollahra in Sydney from 1996 to 1998. Seeking elected office, it seems, is an appealing option for many Australians who have lived and worked in the United States and who view it as a means of using the skills and experience gained from working overseas.

'I could do one of three things: go back and join a large bank, take over SocGen in Australia or stand for Parliament,' Medcraft says. 'It's satisfying at the end of your career to have worked all over the world. You are actually more global, you think so much more broadly than if you've never spent any time overseas. There's a big difference between travelling overseas and living and working overseas.'

People like Medcraft who have lived and worked in the United States for years, accumulating knowledge and experience simply not available in Australia, often come to view their homeland with a more dispassionate eye, gaining the clarity that comes with distance. The dilemma of what to do next — in particular, what will be stimulating professionally — can be persistent and frustrating, but many think not about what Australia has to offer them, but what they have to offer Australia. As has been demonstrated, it is rare for Australian professionals living in America to entirely adopt their new home: nearly all speak fondly of Australia, plan to return one day and have an ongoing involvement in efforts to help other Australian expatriates, whether on a social or a professional level. Many are generous with their time and participate in organisations formed to offer assistance and networking opportunities, such as Los Angeles–based Australians in Film, which has more than 400 members, two-thirds of them expatriates living and working in Los Angeles, and Advance — Australian Professionals in America.

Advance was formed in 2002 as Young Australian Professionals in America and now boasts more than 3000 members. Initially based only in New York, the organisation now has offices in seven US cities and not only offers a means for Australians to meet socially, but also tracks employment opportunities and has a formal mentoring program in different professional disciplines that draws on the skills of executives such as Medcraft, Merrill Lynch's James Gorman; Saatchi & Saatchi's Bob Isherwood and Atria Books' Judith Curr.

'When I first came here, there was virtually no networking amongst Australians,' recalls Bruce Stillman, the CEO of Cold Spring Harbor Laboratory, who is also an Advance mentor. 'I don't think we met any Australians except for running into them at meetings. In the past ten years, maybe as few as the last seven, especially in New York, there's been a lot more networking, organised networking — more trying to help young people who are coming here. You have a common background, and it's nice to be able to talk to Australians.' Effectively tapping into the huge intellectual and financial resource that Australia's expatriate community represents is a recent development.

In its 2004 report into the Australian diaspora for the Lowy Institute for International Policy, authors Michael Fullilove and Chloë Flutter went to great lengths to dispel the commonly held myth that expatriates take more away from Australian than they give back. With some one million Australians estimated to be overseas at any given time, ignoring the potential contribution of about 5 per cent of the national population would seem short-sighted indeed.

'[It] is time for Australian institutions to think seriously about the diaspora,' the report advises. 'The existence of a large community of overseas Australians is relevant to a wide range of issues facing the country and needs to be considered in discussions of those issues. Furthermore, it makes sound economic sense for Australia to increase its efforts to reach out to the diaspora and enmesh them in our national endeavours. First, our diaspora is large. Second, it is strategically situated, both professionally and geographically. Third, there is a deep well of goodwill within the diaspora towards Australia and vice versa. Finally, although the economic consequences of emigration are mixed, there are tangible benefits that can accrue to a home country from its diaspora. Some of these benefits are already flowing to Australia, but by working more closely with our emigrants we can seek to capture more of them.'

Members of the Australian diaspora referred to in the report share a sense of personal responsibility to give something back to their homeland. IBM's Doug Elix has lived in America for a decade. While he remains undecided about whether he will return to his homeland one day, he is convinced of the need for professionals living in the United States to make a contribution to Australia, and of their desire to do so.

'I sincerely hope and passionately believe that the hundreds of thousands of Australians who are overseas think in terms of taking their knowledge back to Australia to help improve the way Australia does business,' Elix says. 'I know plenty of Australians here who want to do that.'

That view is echoed by Merck's David Anstice. (Anstice and Elix are both involved with Advance as mentors.) 'A very common trait I see in the Australians I do meet is that everyone has a very emotional connection to Australia and a strong interest in things Australian,' Anstice says. 'They want to give something back, even from a distance. You have a million professionals working outside Australia: one way to view them is as traitors to the cause, but a much better way is to see them as an asset.'

Capitalising on the unique benefits Australians living and working overseas takes much more than a personal desire to help, however. Some organisations are offering a structured means to take advantage of the diaspora's experience, but experts agree more initiative is needed from the public and private sectors. Fullilove and Futter's Lowy Institute report recommends that the federal government take the lead, arguing that expatriates 'should be seen as an integral element of our diplomatic efforts'.

'A strategically located diaspora can help our international representatives do their job: to gather information, build relationships and advocate Australia's interests,' the report reasons. 'They can also help our public diplomacy effort, serving as goodwill ambassadors and helping to project an accurate and contemporary image overseas.'

Given that many Americans still view Australia through the prism of Paul Hogan's tourism advertisements — a land of tanned outback men in Akubra hats, without a hint of the global, modern and cosmopolitan elements of Australian society — this effort seems long overdue. By the same token, while the prominence of actors such as Nicole Kidman, Naomi Watts, Eric Bana and Russell Crowe keeps Australia in the headlines as a wonderful country in which to live, scant attention is paid to it as a great place to work. At least some responsibility for changing that lies with the Australians working in companies across the United States.

Now that the former Australian giants of American business — men like Geoffrey Bible, Douglas Daft and Jacques Nasser — have moved on, perhaps the most senior executive working in the US is Dow Chemical's Andrew Liveris.

Born in Darwin, Liveris now lives in the small town of Midland, Michigan, also known as 'Dow Town' for the presence of the headquarters of the company that is its lifeblood. His career has taken him to Hong Kong, Bangkok and the United States, and kept him out of Australia for two decades, yet he foresaw none of this when joining Dow Chemical fresh out of university in 1976 with no more than a strong desire to learn and be challenged professionally.

'At that age, you don't imagine you can get to a job like this. So for me it was purely a thirst for knowledge. Australians know that we're a long way away from everywhere, and my particular fascination was for America. I wanted to see the world and be a part of it. Later on it became clear that I was outgrowing the opportunity to return to Australia and wouldn't get a job unless I left Dow. That possibility came up several times, though I would have had to give up a great career to go home. But my initial impetus was to explore the world.'

In 1994, when Liveris was posted by Dow Chemical to run its operations in Hong Kong, his thoughts again returned to Australia. He saw the Hong Kong position as the pinnacle of his career. 'I'm in the job I like, and I'm near to Australia. We still had it in our sights that we were going to move back to Australia. I mean, we had no problem travelling, but we were very family-oriented and I think that's something we've done very well: every year we've gone back at least once — when we were in Hong Kong more than once. So my children know their cousins and uncles and aunts and grand-parents, and that's something we've maintained despite the distance.

'Then we got transferred to Bangkok and then here to the United States. At that time we were still very much of the mindset that we'd be coming back to Australia. I'd had job offers, because I'd been running significant operations in Asia and Australian companies were beginning to take notice, so several times I'd been offered the opportunity to go back to Sydney. I must admit that it was an enduring theme — maybe because we grew up in the outback; maybe it's because we're typical Australians, I don't know, but we're intensely proud of being from Australia and I think, like any Australians, we're ambassadors.'

Liveris did not return to Sydney. It was, he says, testament to the strong lure professional fulfilment represents, especially when you are able to look at your career and believe it is still on an upward trajectory. American companies, he believes, are 'good at doing this: they invest in human talent'.

'It shows how powerful the career motive and the growth aspir-ation was in me that we resisted going back,' Liveris says. 'The lure to go back to the country you love, a city you think is great, to have a nice lifestyle, beach, weather, boat and all that — it was always huge. But the path I was on was one of incredible learning. I was being given increasing responsibilities in this global American corporation. I was doing well. It wasn't even the money: the money was nice, but every job I got was an exciting new adventure. In 1999 I got the call to come back [to the US]. That was the toughest. It was at that point that we finally said, "Look, we'll always be Australian, we'll always return to our family. Our kids are growing up as citizens of the world ... it doesn't really matter where we're physically located." So we bit the bullet. It was at that point that we said we'll probably be staying in the US until I retire. Either that or I get so close to the top job at Dow but I don't get it. And then at that point I'd figure out what to do. That was late 1999, and here we are.'

At 51, Liveris is still young for a chief executive. 'I've arrived at this spot at a fairly good age. Good health willing, I've got myself a couple of decades to do things I really want to do.' Just what he will do once his time at Dow Chemical ends occupies his thoughts, particularly the question of whether he will return to Australia and, if he does, the capacity in which he will return. In the meantime, however, he has a definite short-term priority.

'I want to be a successful CEO of Dow — after investing this many years, to be given this awesome responsibility, who wouldn't give it their all and make it work? — and then see what happens. So I'll see that through for sure. The bigger question, though, concerns my own personal feel of how I see Australia. I view Australia as a country that, especially under its current leader, Prime Minister Howard, is beginning to embrace its place in the world. It's reaching out finally as a nation. It's no longer seen as isolationist but as a country that's engaged in the world.

'I happen to believe that Australians overseas have a desire to — and this includes me — play a role. That role is not abundantly clear; it could mean lots of things. I'm not the type who can just go sit on the beach. I could go back and consider politics. I've always been politically driven, so I could consider running for office. I could see that as a way of giving back. It would be quite something and very possible, instead of the typical people who run for office, to get some of Australia's global diaspora — and not in an arrogant way, not in a threatening way, not in a way that creates a sense of "them and us, they've been overseas and think they know everything", but more to go back and with your global perspective to help Australia take its next leap.'

Liveris is aware that some Australians would view with hostility the idea of someone like him parachuting in from the United States to seek public office. Perhaps many would. Yet such a view appears to be very much in the minority: a survey conducted for the Lowy Institute paper on Australia's diaspora found only one in ten people believed expatriates 'have let us down by leaving Australia', while 91 per cent agreed with the statement that they were 'adventurous people prepared to try their luck and have a go overseas'. So it seems Australians have an overwhelmingly positive view of what might traditionally have been negatively characterised as the 'brain drain'.

'I know those camps, and I characterise myself as somebody who feels like he can be a bridge, because I'm fiercely loyal and patriotic. I am a person who wears Australia on my sleeve. I feel strongly about the attributes of the country and the ability for the country to be a difference maker despite its small population, and if I can in some way contribute my global knowledge to assist Australia in reaching that end, then I will. It wouldn't be with the notion of going back to retire in Australia. It would be with the notion of going back to contribute. I want to and I will contribute, whether through politics or consultancy or running something institutional or academic. I don't care. I want to be able to close the circle. I actually want to be able to introduce into Australia some of America's strengths, such as philanthropy.

'I am exceptionally privileged to be in this role, but I also feel confident in being able to execute it, which tells me that if I keep doing what I'm doing and putting my energy and my passions and my judgement to work, then whatever I choose to do, I can have an impact. If I have to summarise the American model, it is that it allows people to rise to their maximum potential impact. I'd like to be able to keep doing that. If I do another five, six or seven years as Dow's CEO, I've got at least another 10, 12 years to do some more.'

Liveris is passionate about developing Australia's links with its overseas workforce and leveraging that talent base to create opportunities. While he sees many positive changes in the way Australia engages with the rest of the world, he also believes it has a long way to go, while nominating himself as 'willing to be Australia's best ambassador, onshore or offshore'.

'What I'd love to see is that engagement keeping on accelerating. I dare say most of Australia's professional expatriates are exactly in that camp: proud of our country, proud of what it has done, what it has achieved as a young country, proud of our institutions and our constitution, proud of our way of life, proud of our education system, although it's struggling somewhat, proud of our national character, proud of our lack of ego. There's no difference in you saying these things and living in Sydney and me saying them and living in Michigan. So how can I, we, embrace these attributes as global citizens and connect to Australia?'

10 THE WORLD'S BEST FALLBACK POSITION

David Hill had been in London for almost six years pulling together British Sky Broadcasting, the pay television network that revolutionised Europe. Arriving in Britain in 1988, Hill joined Rupert Murdoch's Sky Television, which later merged with British Satellite Broadcasting to create BSkyB. At the end of 1993 he believed the hard work had finally been completed. The company had won the television rights to the English Premier League soccer competition, sending its subscriber numbers through the roof.

'It was making money and on its way to success,' Hill recalls. 'After six years of solid slog in London, of working seven days a week, I said to my wife, "This is great. Now we might get a chance to take the occasional weekend off and explore England, explore Europe. This is going to be terrific." I said, "The back-breaking times are over and life's pretty good." There's an old Roman saying about not telling the gods what you want because they're going to laugh and turn the tables on you.'

In November 1993 Hill received a call from 'the boss', Rupert Murdoch. News Corporation's US free-to-air television network, Fox, had decided to pitch for the broadcast rights to the National Football League, a prize that promised the same impact on the fledgling Fox that winning the Premier League rights had on BSkyB. Murdoch wanted the architect of that success driving the NFL bid and Hill obliged, flying to Los Angeles to prepare the network's pitch. He returned to London and was at the Sky Sports Christmas party when Murdoch called to give him the news: Fox had won.

'So I went home and my wife Joan said, "Did Rupert get you?" and I said, "Yeah." And she said, "What does it mean?" and I said, "Geez, I don't know. Nothing. They'll probably find someone to run it across there and I'll go across and have a chat to him or her about what we should do." Monday came; this happened on the Friday night, and I was getting ready to go down to do a Monday night soccer match — from memory, I think it was Chelsea and Crystal Palace. I was just getting my stuff together when a friend called me from New York and said, "Have you seen the front page of *The Wall Street Journal?*" I said, "How could I? I'm in London." And he said, "You should see it." I said, "Yes, isn't it incredible about Fox getting the NFL!' And he said, "You *really* should see the front page." '

The story in *The Wall Street Journal* began predictably enough: reporting the fact Fox had won the rights to broadcast some NFL games, followed by the nuts and bolts of Murdoch's dealings. Then it got interesting.

'Third paragraph: "Australian-born David Hill is going to be the president of Fox Sports",' Hill recites. 'So I thought, "Holy shit." I called the boss and I said, "Is there anything you want to tell me?" and he said, "Where are you?" I said I was in London and he said, "You better get across to Los Angeles — like, now." So I rang Joan and called the boys and said I'm not doing the soccer tonight, I'm going to LA, and I went home, packed my bags and flew to LA. That was December 1993.'

Hill describes his transfer to the United States as 'a fairly typical story of News Corporation'. It was the culmination of a long journey that began in 1977, at Channel Seven in Melbourne. Kerry Packer had hired some South African cricketers unable to compete internationally because of the International Cricket Conference's suspension of South Africa over its apartheid policy. Two so-called Supertests were played, along with some one-day internationals — it was the start of World Series Cricket, complete with the coloured uniforms, white ball and other unconventional features that now seem normal. One man is responsible for many of the television innovations we today take for granted during cricket coverage, such as placing a camera at each end of the ground: that man is David Hill.

'Sam Chisholm [the head of Channel Nine] called me up in 1977, when I was working at HSV,' Hill recalls. 'He said, "Have you heard of World Series Cricket?" They offered me the job of executive producer. I had never done live television before. I didn't stress that. I didn't say, "I can't do this," but I was so nervous on the first day I vomited walking up the stairs at Waverly Park in Melbourne. I just remember being nervous as shit and vomiting in the stairwell and having the dry heaves.'

Despite the rocky start — for Hill and for World Series Cricket, before it captured the public's imagination — both thrived. Hill oversaw the creation of Nine's *Wide World of Sports*, coordinated Olympic and Logies coverage, did news and produced federal elections. He was producing Nine's America's Cup coverage in Perth in 1987 when Channel Nine's owner, Kerry Packer, telephoned.

'I got a call from Kerry and he said, "What do you think we're worth?" I said, "I think we're worth $550 million." He said that was pretty accurate and I said, "Why on earth are you calling me for a fiscal overview of the network?" And his voice caught and he said, "Son, I've sold us," and I said, "What?" I couldn't imagine us being owned by somebody else. He said, "I've sold us to Alan Bond," and I thought, "Holy shit. Bondy?" And he said, "Yeah, I've sold us for $1.2 billion."

'I was never a huge fan of Alan Bond at all. In fact, I thought he was a crook. I didn't like him. When I got back to Sydney after the America's Cup, it was made plain to me that I was staying for the duration of my contract. The other great attraction was we'd bought the rights to the Winter Olympics in Calgary and I really wanted to do that. So we did the Winter Olympics — that was February 1988 — and I was getting more and more dissatisfied. I really felt I'd done everything I could do in Australia.'

That was when Murdoch came knocking. Hill felt Nine 'wasn't the same without Kerry', so when he was summoned to meet Murdoch in Los Angeles he was intrigued. Murdoch asked him whether he'd like to start a television channel, and when Hill asked when, Murdoch replied: 'When can you get there?'

'I went back to Sydney, said my farewells and very nervously got on a plane to England,' Hill says. 'Of all the gambles I've ever taken in my life and all the risks, that was probably the biggest. No one — friends, colleagues — could understand why I would leave what appeared to be probably the plummest job in Australia, if you're in television. Why you would leave that and start with this huge risky gamble?'

Like many other expatriates, Hill wanted to test himself against the best in the world. He was confident in his ability and had a right to be: BSkyB is now a financial powerhouse, built on the foundation that grabbing the television rights to the Premier League provided. So by 1993, when the challenge arose to drive Fox in a similar way, Hill was ready. Today he is the chief operating officer of DirecTV, yet another Murdoch pay television venture.

Sitting in an office at News Corp's world headquarters in Manhattan, his Australian accent is tinged with an American twang. Hill is proudly Australian but exemplifies that quality common to so many successful Australians overseas: the ability to adapt to his environment. And while he loves his country, after something of a revelation in 2001 he has now become an American citizen.

Although Hill's wife is American and their two children were born in the United States, the thought of taking citizenship had never really been a priority. Yet shortly after the terrorist attacks of September 11, 2001, Hill found himself in New Orleans, the tourist-friendly Louisiana city in America's deep south devastated by Hurricane Katrina last year. He was there to produce coverage of the Super Bowl, the National Football League final that year after year ranks as the country's most watched television event. With the sheer number of eyes advertisers know they will reach, advertising slots sell for more than US$2 million for 30 seconds.

'I had to produce the Super Bowl and I'd planned this very frothy tribute to New Orleans and Mardi Gras and hoopla, and of course all that changed after 9/11,' Hill says. 'It forced me to look at American civilisation, to try to bring out the elements that best represented American civilisation. It was, sort of, my paeon of praise to an adopted country. Everything got back, for me, to the Declaration of Independence. I felt there was this fundamental greatness to the country and the essence of its founding was something to be mar- velled at and wondered at and applauded. I kind of went through this catharsis, doing the show. The lights went out and we sat down and had a beer at the 50-yard line and I thought, "This is now part of me. I can't help it." Even though I feel I'm always an Aussie and I didn't have to give up my Australian citizenship, everything kind of came together and I felt that I needed to [take out US citizenship], not so much for my wife and kids' sakes, but for my sake. I wanted to be part of it.'

Of all the characteristics Australians living and working in New York have in common, the most identifiable and most fiercely defended is their love of their homeland. It's curious: you can talk to Australians who have lived in the United States for two decades, who have American wives and children about to start col- lege, and they will still discuss the possibility of retiring to Australia. When you challenge them to be realistic, the voice drops and the head falls, as if they were silently saying: 'I know, I know. I know I'm staying here forever. But I have to tell myself that I could one day return.'

'All Australians have retained their emotional connection to Aus- tralia,' says Andrew Liveris. 'I am stuck with the notion of keeping my bond. It's important to me, it's important to my family, it's important to our identity. Yes, we are citizens of the world, but we're citizens of the world of the Australian kind. If you have an

American wife, you've cross-married, and you're in another sphere. We're probably at the breach: we can go either way [stay in the United States or return to Australia], but we don't feel pressured by that decision. We're at ease with whatever happens. One thing I've learned is not to overplan your life — it will never be what you plan it to be. There are twists and turns in the road you won't know about. But to retain the emotional commitment, to find ways to make a real contribution of some sort, whether it's here or there, to keep your national identity while being a global citizen, to give your kids a sense of their Australian background even though they've never lived there — those are all things that are not that difficult to do.'

Expatriates work hard to ensure their children — whether born in Australia or in the United States — retain strong ties to their homeland. Most have dual citizenship and carry Australian passports, just as their parents often do. Thanks to changes in citizenship laws in 2002 allowing dual citizenship, no Australian has to make that ultimate sacrifice any more. When Rupert Murdoch took out American citizenship in 1985 to allow News Corp to expand in the United States, he was required to renounce his Australian citizenship.

Retaining those Australian ties has become easier than ever, thanks to the Internet. For a decade Westfield America's Peter Lowy would renew his subscription to the American magazine *Sports Illustrated* every year for a single year; he resisted making a commitment for any longer. Now he can read *Sports Illustrated* and still feel entirely connected to Australia. All the major newspapers are available online, as are instantaneous news updates on everything from politics to sport. American pay television services show the Australian Football League, Australian Rugby League, rugby from around the world and, if you're lucky, cricket. Websites help you buy Tim Tams, Vegemite and sausage rolls. You never have to look far to find another Australian, and this sense of connectedness can only improve with the more widely available E-3 working visa.

'Australia is still very much home,' says Merck & Co's David Anstice. 'I think the lifestyle aspects are as appealing, or even more appealing, after all of these years. I still follow the cricket, the rugby. I get a couple of newspapers a week, as well as *The Bulletin*. My attitude towards Australia is as emotionally strong as it ever was. Every time I go there, I love it. But is Australia doing all it can to be successful in the world? My wife and I worry about the aspirations of people in Australia and whether people are too laid back, which is probably a result of our living in the US too long. We both think it's good to have aspirations and ambitions and we sometimes see Australia as a little too easygoing.'

Lifestyle versus career: it can be a tough choice to make. People who have made the effort to relocate in the United States are necessarily highly motivated and career-driven, which can make the lack of appealing professional options in Australia all the more frustrating. Atria Books publisher Judith Curr says she 'wouldn't move back to Australia to go back into this industry'.

'There'd be no point. If I still wanted to have this involvement in publishing and to work this hard and with these amazing people, I just couldn't — there aren't that many opportunities in Australia. If I went back to work in Australian publishing again with the expectation that it would be the same kind of job I have here, that would be deeply unsatisfying. But if I was self-employed or if I had some kind of financial stake in it that was different from being an employee and that added another element and a new dimension to it, the size of it wouldn't really matter. What would matter would be the reward. If there is a future in being a bi-hemispheric citizen, then you would be able to work in both places. Maybe you can create a new way of doing it. The sun and the surf and the beach and the sand are fabulous, but you don't want to do it every day, and you can go back whenever you want to.'

On moving to the United States in 1996 Curr's initial contract was for three years. 'We thought three to five years, then five to seven, then seven to ten and now we feel like it's open-ended.' As other Australians have done, Curr found that her skills were absolutely transferable to the American market, so why not ride the train as long as you can?

'The worst thing is to go back too soon or to go back for something that doesn't satisfy you,' Curr says. 'I've seen a lot of people make that mistake actually. And then you can't come back here. At this particular point, my career is going really well. With Atria Books, people know what it's all about now. We've been very successful in a short amount of time in a very difficult environment. I always like it if you can succeed when everything is against you, when you put down really good roots for something. I think being in Australia, having gone through those experiences in a small market, prepared me for being in a market that's shrinking. People always say, "How can you compare a small market to this one?" and I say that Australia is the future of American publishing. You have to be much more nimble and much more cost conscious because the market is finite. That helped.'

Perversely, the fact that returning to Australia is always an option allows those in the United States to take risks and endure hardships to a much greater degree than they might otherwise.

'Someone can offer you the best job in Australian journalism, but you do that for five years and what do you do next?' asks *Time* magazine's arts editor, Belinda Luscombe. 'I think Gordon Elliott once said, "Australia is the world's best fallback position". I thought that really sums it up and it makes you braver here, because if everything goes to shite you can just go home and pick up something. It's a fantastic safety net. I think it leads to Australians being more easygoing, because if it all becomes too much, you can just go home.

'But there's a carrot and a stick here in New York. The stick is you have to have some means of getting by. You can't loaf, there's no welfare — it's not like Australia. You can't even get free TV because the reception's so crappy. Everything costs money. You can't live on nothing. Then there's the carrot: the ceiling here is so high; there are great jobs, and people are getting them. You just have to somehow get in. I didn't want to go home not having done anything worthwhile. So we kept sort of staying because there was a lot of potential.'

Luscombe has now been in America since 1991 and shows no signs of returning. 'I'd love to go back. Our intention is to go back, but who knows when or for what? So much of your energy is taken up just getting through the day that in the long term there needs to be some catalyst, I suppose.

'The very last time we had to face the point of "do we go home or do we not?", the reason we didn't was because we still wanted to travel more here and it's a one-way ticket. Once you've been in Australia for a couple of years, it would be extremely hard to come back. The plan now is to just cross each bridge as we come to it and see what happens. I'm not bored yet, so I guess when I get bored or it gets to be a grind, then I'll go back.'

Ros Coffey, the senior vice president and chief administrative officer for finance at investment bank Lehman Brothers, lived in London for six years before coming to New York in 1997. She never planned to be away so long — she kept telling her mum it would be for just two years.

'When I'd been away for four years, I thought I'd never go home. I like to think that I will go back to Australia. In the back of my mind I think I've always known that there will come a time … Australia offers a very different lifestyle and it's a wonderful lifestyle. But you have to be ready for it. I think you have to get some things out of your system.

'Australia is fantastic. There are enough good companies, there's enough industry, there's enough banking, enough commerce, to present good career options for young people. At the same time, you can have a great house, a garden, and you're probably 20 minutes from the beach. That's a fantastic lifestyle. I think it's a wonderful compliment to Australia that you can have both. But I just don't know about the number of senior jobs back home, and I wouldn't be on any radar screens.'

'It's fascinating to pinpoint the first time somebody lands in the place they have moved to and says, "I'm home," ' says Westfield's Peter Lowy. 'I remember it: we were coming back from a trip, Janine and I, and said, "Gee, it's really good to be home." And I looked around and it was LA. It was just a stunning moment. I don't know whether it was after five or six or seven years here. That's when you know you're stuck for a while, when you stop making the one-year or two-year constructs, when you move from the year-to-year to "I'm going to be here for a while".'

For Morgan Stanley's James Gorman, the realisation that America could be home for quite a while came early — after just a couple of years. Having arrived in the United States in 1985, he completed his Master's in Business Administration at Columbia University and landed a job at management consultants McKinsey & Co.

'After I'd been working for two years and my career was in pretty good shape, I realised that if I wanted to, I could stay in the US. I had that option,' Gorman says. 'You only have the option if it's going well on the work front. Your options are much diminished if it's not going so well. And even though we were in a difficult part of the economic cycle, things were going pretty well for me. I thought, if I can do okay in this kind of environment, then in a good environment clearly there's going to be no pressure to send me back. I then realised it was up to me, not my employer, when I wanted to leave. And that balance changes how you look at things.'

By 1990 Gorman had married an American. Following his career at McKinsey, a brief period working in Spain and several years at Merrill Lynch & Co., he has a distinctly global outlook. The question has become not whether to return to Australia but whether to move anywhere else if the work came up. When job offers come from Australia, he describes them as 'no more or less special than job offers you might get to work in the US or Europe'.

'The Australian employment market was not a big draw,' Gorman says. 'It was certainly no better than here, and unarguably it's a lot smaller. Not to take anything away from it — there are tremendous careers to be had in any country. But it could be in Spain, it could be in Australia or it could be in Germany. I'm not necessarily more or less reluctant to walk away for an Australian company. I'm a little blind now to what companies are headquartered where. The family lifestyle drives where you want to live. But a career opportunity? I couldn't care less where it is, whether it's an Australian or a British company. Once you've operated at a global level, that's less important to you.'

Having said that, Gorman is more upbeat than many about the attractiveness of Australia as an employment destination for top executives. 'There are lots of very, very large corporations in Australia. Global corporations, and in financial services there are some very large corporations. There are opportunities. They may not be exactly the same — for example, in the sector I'm in, financial services, there's nothing remotely resembling the private client business I'm with here. But I don't really think about it just in terms of size; it's more in terms of how interesting the job is. In some ways, working something smaller and turning it around can be a very interesting experience.'

Gorman has joined DirecTV's Hill in taking out American citizenship while retaining his Australian passport. His reasoning is entirely logical: he waited until it was possible to have dual citizenship and then decided he wanted to give something back to the country that had been so good to him.

'If you're going to live in another country for 20 years, I think you owe it to them and to yourself to become a citizen, particularly when you can hold dual citizenship,' Gorman says. 'You're paying your taxes, you're a member of the community — you've got to participate in the electoral process. The community here is tremendously supportive in allowing you to live here, and I think you owe them a bit of loyalty back. You know, when I was growing up, if there was a guy down the street who had moved from England 20 years ago and he still hadn't taken out Australian citizenship, you'd say, "What's wrong with you?" You can't have it both ways. The government made it much easier by allowing dual citizenship, so it's hard for me to comprehend anybody being here for a long time and not becoming a dual citizen.'

Belinda Luscombe compares succeeding in corporate America to riding an escalator: 'You get on the bottom step and you don't have to do very much, you just stand there, and eventually you just slowly rise to a certain level. It gets very narrow at the top, but you can get to where I am — upper-middle management, a nice job — just by standing there.'

Once you get to that level, reaching the very top becomes increasingly difficult and perhaps demands more of your time and energy than you're willing to give, so the decision to leave arguably becomes a little easier. It becomes much easier for many with children — not because the US education system is not comparable to Australia's, but because many Australians want their children to enjoy the same lifestyle they did when growing up.

When one-time lipstick entrepreneur Poppy King moved to the United States in 2002, it was a complete relocation. Having endured several tough years professionally as her eponymous cosmetics company struggled to survive, King brought all her furniture with her to the United States, leaving nothing to return to.

'Strangely enough, and as small a detail as it seems, I think that meant a big part of my history was coming with me, and it made me realise I was shifting over here for the foreseeable future,' King says. 'It wasn't just to dip my toe in the water. I knew these type of positions are not something you take up for the short term, especially when you're asked to turn a brand around. A turnaround project is not something that happens overnight.'

Although she gets homesick for certain things — certain people, family and friends; the 'sense of space and just strange things: smells or the light'; the Australian sense of humour — she is enjoying her work too much to consider returning. 'Nothing will ever change the fact that I'm Australian through and through. But I really don't have any long-term plans to return. It's somewhat of a relief to be in a structure as it means, for the first time since I left high school, I don't really have to think too far ahead. I love New York. I'm really beginning to love my job. So I'm taking this time to not really think too far ahead. As a single person without any major family commitments, I can't see any reason why I would move back to Australia. I do see family in my future and then everything becomes open to question. But I think it would be something of a lifestyle choice, and if I were making that I might think about another country before I thought of Australia.'

Among the reasons given for wanting to return home, the Australian lifestyle heads most expatriates' lists. Yet succeeding professionally naturally brings a certain degree of affluence, and wealth facilitates the creation of the lifestyle of your choosing. That is why so many expatriates speak of being bi-hemispheric — splitting their time between Australia and the United States. The *New York Post*'s Col Allan says: 'If I were in a position where I had a huge pile of money and I wasn't working I'd probably spend eight months of the year here and four months of the year down there. But if I wasn't working I'd probably drink myself to death. So I'd prefer to work!'

Judith Curr and her architect husband, Ken Kennedy, have homes in both New York City and the country, as does James Gorman and his wife, who have a house in Duchess County in upstate New York. Gorman describes the suggestion of Australia's superior lifestyle as 'one of the myths that Australians want to perpetuate'.

'There are great lifestyles to be had in Argentina, in France, in the US,' he argues. 'There's a very special type of lifestyle to be had in Australia — which is a very outdoors, sports-driven, beach-driven culture — but there are lots of great lifestyles to be had around the world. We have a phenomenal lifestyle. We live on Central Park, right next to one of the great parks of the world. The kids go to tremendous schools, where the education standard is highly competitive and the education very broad. We're fortunate to have a place in the country and access to all the sports. If we want to take a beach holiday, we can do that at any time of the year. The difference between lifestyles is in Australia it's more relaxed and everybody participates in the lifestyle. In the US it's less relaxed: you've got to be more organised; you can't do things spontaneously. But there are many, many different choices. You've got to be more affluent here in order to participate, but if you're affluent and plan well, you can have the best lifestyle of anywhere in the world. In Australia you can be less affluent, less well organised and still have a very good lifestyle. I guess that's the distinction.'

Ian Phillips, the former executive vice president and general manager of the Commonwealth Bank's US operation, agrees money can buy you a nice American lifestyle. However, while he lived in suburban Scarsdale, just north of Manhattan, before his return to Sydney in 2003, he found there were difficulties in taking advantage of all the area had to offer.

'In the summertime in Manhattan it was horrible. You really need to have an escape,' Phillips says. 'We were very lucky because my wife's aunt lived upstate at a place called Greenwood Lake and we had the run of the place — we could go there whenever we wanted. But you need money to have that lifestyle, absolutely. We lived in Scarsdale and a lot of our neighbours had houses out in the Hamptons and we'd get invited out there all the time. I'd always make excuses not to go, because you'd go out there for a couple of days and you'd go crazy and end up even more stressed from the drive back home on a Sunday. I used to say, "As soon as you get a helicopter to take us out there, we'll come."'

Gorman admits the Australian lifestyle has a unique allure. 'If you're born and bred as an Australian, there's no question that the particular lifestyle is unique and special and strikes a chord with you that will never go away. I was in Sydney recently and went down to Bondi Beach for a swim like any other tourist, but I feel as though I felt the saltwater differently from any other tourist. When I go on the Great Ocean Road on the south coast of Victoria, there's a certain specialness and the fact it's so uncrowded and Australians are so relaxed … there's a natural affinity. I could slip into the Australian lifestyle tomorrow with no problem.

'People would always ask me, "Do you think you'll go back to Australia?" and I would say, 'Not particularly. It's easier for me to stay here than for Penny and the kids to move. It's easier for me to stay than to move. And now, of course, it's been 20 years.'

Gorman gets back to Australia on average twice a year and believes it is much more likely that his family will spend chunks of time there rather than return permanently.

'I don't plan to go back. Could it happen? It's possible. I'd like to see our kids have part of their education there. I'd like to take some extended periods off and travel around Australia. We might end up owning some property down there, keep connected that way. Physically moving is less important to me than being connected. It's more the practicalities of it: to go back would be an enormous disruption to our life. I could perhaps get a comparable job down there — there aren't many — so you're not going back solely for career reasons. I'm lucky in that I don't need to move there in order to see Australia. I've been going down there every eight months for 20 years … a lot of people don't have that flexibility. I have less pressure or sense of need to move there to be connected formally. I'm very lucky really in that regard.'

Curr and Kennedy also go home often. Both have large families and both sets of parents are still alive. Having come to the United States around the age of 40 meant they have close friendships they want to maintain. 'And I get homesick for the weather,' Curr says.

'Come February, I really miss the sunshine. I've decided that I'm bi-hemispheric. I used to feel like every time I went home people would say, "When are you coming home? When are you going to move back?" That was the first three years or so, and I'd say, "Maybe two more years." Then when we would come back here, people would want to know if we were leaving or going to stay. People always wanted to know if we were coming or going. Once I realised we didn't have to make a commitment one way or the other and could actually live equally in both places — have a social life in one and a working life in the other — it made it so much easier for me. I've not left there and I haven't left here — they can co-exist. New York is much closer to Sydney than Sydney is to New York, because everybody comes to New York, which is nice.'

Many Australians express surprise that they have managed to live so happily in the United States, which is perhaps itself an acknowledgement that the American lifestyle is not so bad as to continually remind them of Australia's superiority. 'I never thought it would be this long,' said Los Angeles–based television producer Greg Coote. 'I didn't think I would be washed up on the beach in Laguna.'

Bruce Stillman, CEO of Cold Spring Harbor Laboratory, took his American wife-to-be to Australia before they married: 'I said to Grace, "You should go and see Australia. At least you should see it before we get married so you can have some choice in this."

'The only thing she didn't like about it was the fact that Christmas was in the middle of summer. I think it would have been difficult for her to move to Australia, but it would have to be a very unusual job for me to go back to Australia now. The lifestyle here is very good. I mean, the lifestyle in Australia is fantastic but the fact is I live in the president's house here — it's a beautiful house on the water — yet we're just an hour from New York City, which is really quite amazing.'

Stillman has lived in the United States since 1979. Initially it was going to be just two years. He lives in Cold Spring, a picturesque town north of New York City.

'I didn't choose to come and stay here. In fact, it was quite a big decision to do that,' he says. 'Once you start having kids and they grow up here, it becomes increasingly difficult to return to Australia. But living out here is like living in the suburbs of Sydney. I often think with a view like this — the view from our house is not dissimilar from looking over Middle Harbour or something like that — it's actually quite extraordinary.'

David Hill, now an American citizen, has lived here for 12 years. He met his wife, then a banker with Citibank in Arizona, on a Bollinger champagne-quaffing helicopter ride after the America's Cup. 'It's one of the great stories of all time. I met her on the helicopter, we got chatting, one thing led to another and we ended up getting married and having kids,' Hill says with a laugh. 'It was a total fluke.'

Hill still experiences professional misgivings, even as he enters his sixties and approaches what is normally regarded as retirement age. When he first left Australia, and even when he later left London, he found it hard to cut ties to home, which he ascribes to a habitual conviction he was 'going to be sacked in three months'.

'Every job I've ever had, I've always been terrified and always thought I'd be overwhelmed by it,' he says. 'I've never been one to plan the future. When I left Australia, and again when I left London, I didn't sell my house. I knew that if everything went terribly wrong or pear-shaped, I'd have a little hidey-hole to go sliding back to.' Both houses have since been sold.

'I love doing what I'm doing,' Hill says. 'Mentally it's very rewarding. I can't see myself doing anything in Australia. The only thing I'd want to do in Australia, and this is going to sound really ridiculous: I would love to go back and run the ABC for two or three years. Go in there and kick some arse big time and try to turn it into something that's truly representative of Australian culture.

'But the work's here. When we [the Australian Irregulars in Los Angeles] all sit down, which we do far too infrequently, we find we are very similar. It's no wonder we're all friends. I think that what I felt, although not consciously, when I left was I wanted to prove myself on a larger playing field. I guess we all wanted to prove ourselves working on a world-class playing field. Some of us made it, some of us didn't. That's life. But then it gets back to the question: how do you define making it? All that metaphysical bullshit.'

Now heading towards the age of 60, Hill finds himself more reflective. He has no plans to retire, and thoughts of returning home are remote. 'My problem is that I've been away for 20 years and my friends are now here. The guys that I hang with are all either British or American. I've got two Aussie mates who are literally around the corner, but the rest of my mates are all Americans.

'I can remember Dad going on about retiring from the age of 50. I could no more think of retiring than flying to the moon. It's very odd. Very odd. We don't see ourselves as old despite the damning physical evidence we see every morning in the mirror. I don't know what the hell it is. All of us are of a similar vintage, and none of us, no one's saying, "I'm looking forward to retiring."

'I am getting a hankering ... I'm thinking of buying a block of bush for my kids. I'm feeling the need as I get on to leave a piece of Australia to them, even if it's like 20 acres in the back of Woop Woop. I'm just going to say, especially to the two younger ones who are American — Australian-Americans, I beg your pardon — that there's a piece of Australia with your name on it.'

That nagging sense that Australia is where you truly belong is not unusual. Australians living and working in the United States may enjoy tremendous professional success. They may marry Americans and build new lives. If they're lucky, they can escape the big city for weekends at the beach or in the mountains, and enjoy regular holidays to Australia. Yet the soundness or otherwise of the decision to leave their homeland behind is always open to debate — the doubt never fully dissipates. In the end, it seems you simply need to accept that the two countries, for all their similarities, are very different. To compare them is simply unfair.

'I will say this,' says photographer Ben Watts, who has lived in America for a decade. 'When I go back to Australia now I see so many people with a lot of talent who have stayed and they're very happy. They've got families, they've got a lifestyle. So long as you're content. If you're in the right mind space it's fine. But it's not for everybody. It's just where your head's at.

'I've been chasing a dream and they've already achieved theirs. I was down in Australia at Christmas and I'd like to live back there. But at the moment I've still got the fire. It's about timing, being in the right place at the right time. The last three years I've been getting back there and I intend to do so even more. I worked my arse off last year and I couldn't wait to get to Australia and blow off some steam. I just miss the laid-backness of it. I miss the lifestyle.'

At the end of the day, Australia will be perceived by many expatriates as a lifestyle choice, and that's not meant as an insult. The fact that so many desperately miss the country's unique blend of work and play is a compliment, as is the distinction DirecTV's Hill, among others, draws between America and Australia.

'There is a different ethos between Americans and Australians,' he believes. 'In Australia, people work to live; here, people live to work. Now I've proved to myself what I wanted to prove. I go back and I talk to my brothers and look at my friends — both my brothers are teachers and get scads of holidays, while I'm lucky to get two weeks a year — and who the hell has made the right choice? Materially I'm much better off, but psychologically and in terms of quality of life, I'm not sure. I don't know if all these expatriates spinning around the world are actually smarter, as Peter Allen put it. Who is really smarter — those of us who left and are trying to make it in a broader sense? Or those who stayed?'

ACKNOWLEDGEMENTS

During the preparation of this book over the northern summer of 2005 I was fortunate to be granted extended interviews with Col Allan, David Anstice, Geoffrey Bible, Kay Binnie, Ros Coffey, Greg Coote, Judith Curr, Doug Elix, David Evans, James Gorman, David Hill, Bob Isherwood, Ken Kennedy, Poppy King, Andrew Liveris, Peter Lowy, Belinda Luscombe, Guy and Robyn McKanna, Greg Medcraft, Ian Phillips, Fred Schepisi, Bruce Stillman and Ben Watts. All quotes by these individuals are drawn from the resulting interviews. Jac Nasser's quotes are from an interview I conducted with him for a story published in *AFR BOSS* in November 2003. Sarah Murdoch's comments are extracted from my June 2005 interview with her on behalf of *WHO* magazine. Excerpts from the Lowy Institute report on Australians working overseas, quoted in chapter 9, come from *Diaspora — the World Wide Web of Australians* by Michael Fullilove and Chloë Flutter, © 2004, Lowy Institute, pages 38–39, 43, 46. Thank you to Elena Douglas at Advance — Australian Professionals in America for help in contacting Australian expatriates. Finally, thank you to my friend, photographer Nola Lopez, for your generosity.

INDEX